Part I
My True Identity

and

Part II
In HIM—
so much MORE…!

Apostle Harriet Sleigh PhD

Copyright © 2011 by Apostle Harriet Sleigh PhD
ISBN: 978-0-9566864-3-5

Part 1, My True Identity, first published in 2004.

The moral right of the author has been asserted in accordance
with the Copyright, Designs, and Patents Act 1988.

All rights reserved solely by the author. No part of this publication may be reproduced or transmitted in any form or by any means, electronic or mechanical, including photocopy, recording, or any information storage and retrieval system, without permission in writing from the author

All scripture quotations, except where otherwise labelled, are from the *New King James Version* copyright © 1984 by Thomas nelson, Inc.

This edition is published by:

SUNESIS PUBLICATIONS

For more information about Sunesis Publications, please visit:

WWW.STUARTPATTICO.COM

**To order additional copies of this book, please use the contact details
found on the author's website - www.burningbushrevival.org**

Contents

Part I, My True Identity 1

Part II, In HIM, so much MORE! 57

Part I

My True Identity

Foreword

(to My True Identity)

The life that Jesus Christ came to give us is not bland, boring or dry. It is full of vibrancy, excitement and joy. In other words, Jesus came so we might have genuine fullness of life. That life is like a seed within every born-again Christian. For a person to grow spiritually that life must be appropriated and lived out. A person is transformed by the growth of that life within them. It is not mere intellectual knowledge that transforms a person, it is the revelation of biblical truth by the Holy Spirit in a person's inner being that brings that new life out into the open. The crucifixion, death and resurrection of Jesus Christ have opened up for us a river of new life that is available to all. But we need to learn how to take hold and live in the good of what Jesus has made available to us. In my own life and ministry I have seen the transforming power of God operate through His Word and I know what riches lie in the pages of the bible. In these booklets, Harriet Sleigh provides invaluable tools for the Christian to grow in his or her spiritual life. The principles of scriptural meditation and confession are fundamental to appropriating the life contained in the bible. I encourage you to make full use of these materials and take hold of the abundant life that Jesus died to give you.

Colin Urquhart

My True Identity

Contents

Foreword 3

Chapter 1 Eating the Word 7

Chapter 2. Loved 14

Chapter 3. The Old Has Gone 17

Chapter 4. My New Self 21

Chapter 5. Authority 29

Chapter 6. Walk 36

Chapter 7. Purpose 45

Chapter 8. How to live a scripture 48

1

EATING THE WORD

That which you hold in your hand can transform you to live and walk as Jesus did. God has a glorious purpose for each of His precious children, free from every bondage, walking in the miraculous, in whatever specific area He has called you. How can this be realized? Our growth is dependent on two factors.

Firstly, it depends on the extent to which we want to grow, for Him to increase and us to decrease. If you are content with how you are, do not read on. But if you have a longing from deep within, to live the abundant life He has for you, this is for you.

Secondly, it depends on how much of the Word we yield to so that it takes dominion in our lives, and we live it. Knowing the scriptures just in our minds will have some affect. But it is only if we delight in it, embrace it, letting it affect our whole being, soul and body, and **then live it**, that we truly enter into the abundant life God longs for each of us to walk in.

Scripture clearly tells us that there is a direct relationship between how much we meditate on the Word, and our success (Josh. 1:8). It is our choice, our responsibility. Through spending time with the Word, in the Word, we come to know it is true on the inside of us. Israel was God's chosen nation, but a generation of them failed to reach the Promised Land because of unbelief (Heb 3; 19). It is knowing the truth in our hearts **within** that sets us free. This life is not a struggle. Praise God it has already been won for us on the cross. As born-again believers, we are now in the Promised Land. We are one with Him as a branch is to a vine. We do not have to fight to possess the promises, but to **discover** what is ours and live it.

As long as we identify with the person we used to be, our old nature,—'I' have always been like this, although I want to change', our Christian life will be a struggle. This old 'I' is defined by those around us and ourselves. It is essentially separate from God. I may try my hardest to change and become more like Jesus, but make slow progress. This is the traditional way of thinking. It is in fact 'Old Covenant' way of thinking. It involves operating through the tree of the knowledge of good and evil, where the enemy has full access. We evaluate what we have done with criteria independent of God. The enemy, with joy points out where we have failed. He reinforces our deficiency—'You will never make it', or 'It will not work for you'. It is so easy to feel condemned; then to say the Word does not work, and to justify our failure.

Glory to God, Jesus has set us free, not because of what we have done but because of His shed blood on the cross. The veil separating man from the Father has been destroyed. When Jesus died it was torn in two from top to bottom (Matt 27:51), the old 'I' was crucified with Him and He has given us a new 'I'. I have a new identity, as His child, born of the Word of God. My unique personality, has received His righteousness, His nature. I have it **now**, with all of His life, His love, joy peace, power etc; now I can live in His presence. I am no longer separate from Him, but abide in Him as a branch does of a vine. It would be madness for a branch to frequently separate itself and then try to rejoin the vine. Similarly for us to see ourselves as separate and then seek God to come into His presence. We are there **now**, all the time. There is no reason to leave. Is this possible? How could this work for me? The essence of this new life is seeing ourselves as having a new 'I' who is no longer separate, but in constant living relationship with the Father, Jesus the Word, and the Holy Spirit.

We are told how this can become a reality for each of us. 'Be transformed by the renewing of our minds', (Rom 12:2). The word transformed in Greek is 'metamorphoo', the word used to describe the extraordinary transformation of a caterpillar into a butterfly. This analogy may help us to understand and live in this glorious truth of what He has done for us on the cross. We used to be limited and earth-bound, as is a caterpillar. But He has made us into new creations, or a new species, as different from what we used to be as a butterfly is from a caterpillar. 'If anyone is in Christ, he is a new creation; old things have passed away; behold all things have become new', (2Cor 5:17). The tenses show us that this is not a promise but a description of what He has made us, of what we are now.

We are changed as we believe this, let go the old 'caterpillar' mindset, and replace it with that of a 'butterfly' or new creation. The illustration is evocative. A caterpillar crawls with its many legs, is vulnerable to predators, totally earth-bound, and lives its life chewing, struggling. Similarly we used to be self-centred, limited to our natural senses—what we could see or hear etc: Fear was an unwanted companion, fear of not being able to manage, fear of the problems, fear of the future, fear of what others think of us. We are no longer 'caterpillars', but 'butterflies'. The very life of God is in us. Butterflies spend much of their time resting unperturbed. They are not limited by natural laws like the law of gravity, but fly displaying their beauty with which God has clothed them. Glory to God. Similarly when we discover our inheritance, we can rest in it. Struggling is over. We learn how to fly, how to operate in God's supernatural ways, His protection, His supply, divine health, freedom from fear etc: The enemy is beneath our feet, he is defeated, he cannot touch us unless we open the door to him. His only access to us is through our minds. As we learn to fill our minds with the word of God and refuse to give him, with his negative thoughts, any place, he cannot touch us. I begin to speak of myself as my true 'butterfly' identity' 'I am a new creation; I am delivered from the power of darkness'. The Bible, particularly in the epistles, describes our life, the glorious life of the new creation. What He asks us to do He enables. Through the **living Word living in us**, each one of us can 'be', and 'do' all that the Word describes.

The Word has within it inherent power, the awesome power of God to create or accomplish whatever He desires. The Word spoken by God created the world. He sent His Word and healed people. His prophets spoke and kings trembled. Jesus was and is the Word of God. He, who we love, in the form of the Word, is living and powerful, sharper than any two-edged sword. In Acts we are told the Word grew mightily and prevailed. The Holy Scriptures are 'able to make you wise', (2Tim 3:15). God is seeking people who tremble at His Word; see its awesome power and yet are drawn to it as a lover is to His beloved. The Holy Spirit, who lives in every born-again believer, is our teacher. He longs to receive the Word, embrace it, so that it vibrates in our hearts, revealing to each of us new glorious revelations, which can ignite within and so transform us, particularly as we step out in faith and live it.

He wants us to **have a beautiful relationship** with Him in many ways, as Lord, Father, husband, friend, and also as the Word, because He is the Word. We are told to love Him with all our heart, with all our soul and with all our strength (Deut 6:5; and Matt 22:37). If we love Him we love the living Word. We can have a love relationship with the Word. As Jeremiah said, 'Your words were found and I ate them. And your word was to me the joy and rejoicing of my heart' (Jer.15:16). We are told to draw water from the well of salvation within with joy. With joy we embrace the Word, because we love Him.

We know that the transformation will be glorious; that He will enable each of us to walk in His anointing, His presence, and in His presence is fullness of joy. This can be a reality for us. See yourself living like this. Let this be your personal vision. 'Without vision my people perish', but with it they have a glorious zeal for life. The scripture says that Jesus stood out, in that He had more joy than all his companions.

'As He is so are we in the world', (1John 4:17) — this calling is for each of us. When this describes you and me, ordinary believers, our lives will be radiant; they will 'be' revival. Every nation will be impacted.

How much do we believe? The amount that we live! Only as we live the new creation life, which He has purchased for us, will He be glorified. We are called to leave the old 'caterpillar' life and **delight in being** a 'butterfly'. We will find it works. It will give us a new zeal for life. Enthusiasm means 'in God'. Being a 'butterfly' will change our expectations; we know that God will be continually intervening on our behalf in glorious ways. It will affect the way we talk and the way we behave. Below is described a way that will mightily assist in enabling you and me to walk just as Jesus did — to get to know and live in our **'true identity'** — Hallelujah!

This is followed by a section called, **'How to live a scripture'**, which will help you to digest and live a particular scripture which has impacted you.

HOW?

By declaring and meditating on who I am and what I can do as a new creation, as described in the scriptures. This is **MY TRUE IDENTITY**, the 'butterfly' life, God ordained for me—hallelujah!

It includes confessions about,

How I am loved passionately by Almighty God,
The awesome power of the cross, how I am set free from the past,
Our new self or new identity—glory to God, I am a blessing,
The authority that is now mine,
The day to day walk He expects of every believer, aglow and burning in the Spirit,
His purpose now embedded in my heart—to glorify our Lord.

By speaking them out regularly and meditating on them, they will become a reality, the way you see yourself, think, and respond whatever the circumstances. Also some of the scriptures are included from which they emerged. Spending time in them will reveal marvellous other dimensions of the truth and so increase your understanding. You will be challenged to delight in finding others to reveal more and more.

As a man thinks in his heart so is he. Your mindset will change to automatically think the truth about yourself as described in the Word. The old negative fearful 'caterpillar' mindset will be replaced by a vibrant, positive glorious one, of who you really are, and God's unique purposes for you. The Holy Spirit will change you, from glory to glory.

There are so many ways that the following declarations can be used to digest these precious truths. They are in large bold to make them easier to read. You could speak some or all of them out, every day. If you do it before you go to sleep your spirit will continue to take hold of them while you sleep. I have found when doing this I sometimes wake up with a glorious revelation—wow! Sometimes I go through them asking God to whisper to me something new about each one, before I go on to the next. I may only 'eat' a few. Next time I can continue.

I may speak them out until I come to one that touches my heart and start praying it for myself or for others. The scriptures are there to help the 'feast'. It does not matter which way or ways you choose; it is regularly speaking and meditating on them that will enable the Holy Spirit to take hold of the truth and impact the way you see yourself. Even after one week you will be conscious of a difference. After a month the change will be distinctive. After six months it will be the natural way you think. After that God will continue to reveal more and more of His secrets and mysteries; there is no limit.

The Holy Spirit delights in revealing special insights to each one of us. I share some He has given me in order to encourage you, brother sister, to let Him whisper and reveal glorious facets of the scripture you are feasting on. He longs to do this for you . . . and to walk in it Glory to God!

MY TRUE IDENTITY

**Most assuredly, I say to you, unless one is born again,
he cannot see the kingdom of God** (John 3:3).

This applies to everyone, whether living on the streets or in a mansion, illiterate or the most learned. No matter how educated we may be, we need to be born again. God made us in His image. He made us to know Him and through this to live a blessed abundant life. Deep within each one of us is the real heart, our spirit that longs to know God. Through our education we build up many barriers, ideas about ourselves of who we want to be or think we are. We may be very successful in worldly terms, yet inside we know there is more to life. Religion has focused on aspects of ourselves like our past, our qualities, our problems, which in fact draw attention to our old 'caterpillar' selves and away from God. He wants to go straight to our heart and meet us there. Glory to God, when we respond, we find that the other problems, the self issues, melt away as we come to know that Almighty God loves us, and longs to do glorious things in and through our lives.

Many know about God, but do you know God, know of his love for you? If not, or you are not sure, right now decide that 'This is for me'. It is only when you are born again that your eyes are open and you are able to see and step into the glorious truths. Be sure you have responded from your heart to His invitation and receive His life.

> **'For God so loved the world that he gave his only begotten Son, that whoever believes in him should not perish but have everlasting life.'** (John 3:16)

> 'Forgive me Lord, I want to live my life for You alone'.
> **I am saved, born again.**

2

LOVED

Christianity is a beautiful love relationship between us and our Lord. We step from knowing that God loves us because the bible says so, to experiencing it as a glorious ongoing reality. This love relationship is as in marriage. Intimate knowledge of our Lord is acquired. We get to know His heart, His will for us and the joy of living our lives as He directs. It motivates us, instils in us a hunger to know and serve Him more and more. As we get to know Him, He becomes increasingly our security. **Our** confidence in Him grows, so that we know He will not let us down as we do whatever He asks of us. The first commandment is to love Him with all our heart, soul, strength and mind, so that this can be a reality in our lives.

I had not been a Christian for long, when I found the verse, 1Peter 1:8, which reads, 'whom having not seen you love. Though now you do not see Him, yet believing, you rejoice with joy inexpressible and full of glory'. At that time things were not going too well for me and I thought, I would like to have that 'joy unspeakable'. What are the conditions? To love and believe in Him. I do believe, so the issue was truly loving Him. If I was in love with someone, I would be thinking of that person all the time, delighting in them, going over precious moments. I decided to do that with my Lord. I remember walking to a neighbouring farm, saying, with enthusiasm, 'I love You'. I had a distinct warm feeling inside, which I now realize was the Spirit within me delighting in my heart. I walked across the field with a spring in my step— hallelujah! He was encouraging me. The more I thought of Him, and my heart whispered endearments to Him, the more joy welled up from within. When having to do something boring, like a household chore, I would tell Him of my love and that I was doing it for Him, and it no longer was a chore! Now, whatever the circumstance, I know a joy inside. I can love Him always, be in His presence, and the scripture says, in His presence is fullness of joy.

Declarations

1John 4:18 There is no fear in love; but perfect love casts out fear, because fear involves torment. But he who fears has not been made perfect in love.
I am loved perfectly
(I know every detail; your strengths, weaknesses, the past, the future. Trust Me; I want to bless you).

Rom 8:15 For you did not receive the spirit of bondage again to fear, but you received the Spirit of adoption by whom we cry out, 'Abba Father.'
I am loved intimately—'abba' Father
(The veil is torn, be so open with Me, trust, delight in My embrace).

Is 54:5 For your Maker is your husband, the Lord of hosts is His name; and your Redeemer is the Holy One of Israel; He is called the God of the whole earth.
—as by a perfect husband
(As the closest love relationship, as 'one'. Let it be, 'we' doing . . . .)

S of S 8:6-7 Set me as a seal upon your heart, for love is as strong as death, jealousy as cruel as the grave; its flames are flames of fire, a most vehement flame. Many waters cannot quench love, nor can the floods drown it. If a man would give for love all the wealth of his house, it would be utterly despised.
I am loved passionately as with the very flame of the Lord
(Nothing reserved or held back).

Rom 8:38-39   For I am persuaded that neither death nor life, nor angels nor principalities nor powers, nor things present nor things to come, nor height nor depth, nor any other created thing, shall be able to separate us from the love of God which is in Christ Jesus our Lord.
I cannot be separated from Your love
(Whatever the circumstances—no mountain too high or valley too low, I am there with you).

Eph 1:4   Just as He chose us in Him before the foundation of the world, that we should be holy and without blame before Him in love.
I was chosen before the foundation of the world
(You are unique. I have a special glorious purpose already planned for you).

3

THE OLD HAS GONE

The power of the cross is so glorious. I am free from my past. It is no longer part of me. I do not need deliverance or healing. I am the delivered, the healed. When I look back on it I do so with thanks in my heart—hallelujah!

I am loved perfectly. His hand was on every part of my life; even the tragedies. I went through many hard times. I was unwanted. I married and had two children that died. My husband left me. I learnt so much from Joseph's life. He went through much hardship, totally rejected by his brothers, as a slave and then years in prison, before he became ruler of Egypt. But, he was then able to look back on the past and see it from God's perspective; I believe, with thanks in his heart. 'God sent me before you to preserve life . . . it was not you who sent me here but God'; and he has made me a father to Pharaoh, and lord of all his house, and ruler throughout all the land of Egypt' (Gen 45:5, 8).

I wanted to be free from my past. I had to first forgive all those involved; my mother, the doctors, my ex husband. But it was through seeing them as Joseph had done from God's perspective that enabled a total release. The past had to be redefined, so I could even thank Him for the traumatic events. For example, I know I was unwanted by my parents, but that was irrelevant because I was wanted by my heavenly Father. What comfort I can bring to others who have been unwanted. Because two of my children died I see the preciousness of life etc: Now when I look back on the past there are no negatives, no weight. I am free.

So many Christians live their lives trying to be free from their past, not realizing it has already been done for them on the cross.

This is the truth. This is what we are saved from. We are free from being self-centred struggling 'caterpillars'. We are in fact, more than the delivered, or the healed. That person we used to be is no more. Now we can live our lives as new creations, as glorious 'butterflies'.

Declarations

Rom 6:3-6   Or do you not know that as many of us as were baptized into Christ Jesus were baptized into his death? Therefore we were buried with Him through baptism into death, that just as Christ was raised from the dead by the glory of the Father, even so we also should walk in newness of life. For if we have been united together in the likeness of His death, certainly we also shall be in the likeness of His resurrection, knowing this that our old man was crucified with Him, that the body of sin might be done away with . . .

2Cor 5:17   Therefore, if anyone is in Christ, he is a new creation; old things have passed away; behold all things have become new.

Gal 2:20   I have been crucified with Christ; it is no longer I who live, but Christ lives in me; and the life which I now live in the flesh I live by faith in the Son of God who loved me and gave Himself for me.

I(old self centred 'I')have been crucified with Christ (The person you used to be is no more, that old self-centred independent person full of fear, pride, was buried with Me. When I rose from the dead, so did you as a new creation, a new person).

Is 43:1   But now, thus says the Lord, who created you, O Jacob, and He who formed you, O Israel: 'Fear not, for I have redeemed you; I have called you by your name; you are Mine.

Gal 3:13   Christ has redeemed us from the curse of the law, having become a curse for us (for it is written, "Cursed is everyone who hands on a tree")

Eph 1:7   In Him we have redemption through His blood, the forgiveness of sins, according to the riches of His grace.

My True Identity

                I (new 'I') have been redeemed through Your blood
                (It is a perfect redemption. You are free from all the bondages of the curse—fear, oppression, negatives).

Col 1:13   He has delivered us from the power of darkness and conveyed us into the kingdom of the Son of His love,
I have been delivered from the power of darkness
(As if you no longer lived in the same country; now you are in a new country, new language, new joys).

Phil 3:20   For our citizenship is in heaven, from which we also eagerly wait for the Savior, the Lord Jesus Christ,

Is 33:24   And the inhabitant (of Zion) will not say, "I am sick"; the people who dwell in it will be forgiven their iniquity.
I am a citizen of Zion
(Love, peace and joy have replaced fear, darkness, sickness, failure, which are now foreign to you.)

2Tim 1:7   For God has not given us a spirit of fear, but of power and of love and of a sound mind.

1John 4:18   There is no fear in love; but perfect love casts our fear, because fear involves torment. But he who fears has not been made perfect in love.
I do not fear
(You are free from the fear of man and the need to worry. My perfect love and power has replaced it. Your security is now in Me, so in its place, delight in an awesome fear of Me).

Rom 6:14   For sin shall not have dominion over you, for you are not under law but under grace.

Rom 8:2   For the law of the Spirit of life in Christ Jesus has made me free from the law of sin and death.
I am not under the law but under grace
(The weight of striving to please Me, of failure and success, is now replaced by a delight in doing

Is 53:4-5   Surely He has borne our sicknesses and carried our pains; yet we esteemed Him stricken, smitten by God, and afflicted. But He was wounded for our transgressions, He was bruised for our iniquities; the chastisement for our peace was upon Him, and by His stripes we are healed.

1Pet 2:24   Who Himself bore our sins in is own body on the tree, that we, having died to sins, might live for righteousness — by whose stripes you were healed.

I have been healed
(The body that used to be sick is no more. Now you have the same Divine nature that I have. As I was when on earth, you too are free from sickness, depression, confusion, the past etc).

Is 10:27   It shall come to pass in that day that his burden will be taken away from your shoulder, and his yoke from your neck, and the yoke will be destroyed because of the anointing oil.

Gal 5:1   Stand fast therefore in the liberty by which Christ has made us free, and do not be entangled again with a yoke of bondage.

I am free from every bondage
(I shed My blood because I love you, to cut you loose from your culture, sin, yourself etc; so you are free to know Me).

Rom 8:1   There is therefore now no condemnation to those who are in Christ Jesus, who do not walk according to the flesh, but according to the Spirit.

I am free from condemnation
(Know that that nagging accusation is from the enemy and give it no place).

4

MY NEW SELF

He has made us new creations, a new species, as butterflies are different from caterpillars—hallelujah! It is a glorious truth that we are no longer ordinary people, but the very life of God is throbbing through our bodies. We are born again of the living Word of God, the incorruptible divine seed. The Holy Spirit now vitalizes our mortal bodies. Many Christians live a life trying to become what God has already made them. We just need to believe it, live it, and let go the old mindset. So many have received the lie from the pit that they are of no or very limited value. They therefore expect little from life. The truth is each of us is unique, and so special to our Lord. He has chosen each of us for a glorious purpose.

What a joy it has been to see hundreds of people in Africa and India, who saw themselves as with no hope, no future, forgotten by the world, be transformed by realizing that God had a mighty purpose for them which they could step into. When they give their lives to Jesus, and are filled with the Holy Spirit, their sad faces are transformed; zeal and joy radiate through their eyes.

I easily identify with such people because I saw myself as being of little value. I remember seeing from the scripture (Gen 12:2), that not only was I blessed, but a blessing. The last thing I saw myself was as a blessing. I remember deciding to take hold of this truth and spoke it out often. After a few days, something within agreed with my words. The challenge was then to live it, to release it. It was a decision. Instead of shrinking when with others, deciding I was going to bless them, with what I said, with a smile, joy or whatever. To my delight I found it worked. What a joy it is to bless. It is so true that it is better to give than to receive, totally contrary to our self-centred society which is all out to get. The more we give, the more He pours into us to give—hallelujah! Confessing the truth did not change me into a butterfly, the truth welled up inside, and the old way of thinking fell away. I was not trying to bless, but being a blessing, releasing what was inside of me. There is such a difference, it is **knowing the truth inside** that makes us free.

Declarations

Gen 12:2   I will make you a great nation; I will bless you and make your name great; and you shall be a blessing.

Eph 1:3   Blessed be the God and Father of our Lord Jesus Christ, who has blessed us with every spiritual blessing in the heavenly places in Christ.
I am a blessing
(Your new nature has been so mightily blessed with every spiritual blessing. Let them flow naturally from you).

Eph 2:8   For by grace you have been saved through faith, and that not of yourselves, it is the gift of God.
I live in grace
(Our life is a love relationship; such joy in your heart because you know that My grace will enable you to do whatever I ask of you).

1Pet 1:23   having been born again, not of corruptible seed but incorruptible, through the word of God which lives and abides forever.

Rom 8:11   But if the Spirit of Him who raised Jesus from the dead dwells in you, He who raised Christ from the dead will also give life to your mortal bodies through His Spirit who dwells in you.
I have been born again through the Divine incorruptible seed of the Word of God
(Your whole being, including your mortal body throbs with My life).

My True Identity

1Cor 15:45   Thus it is written, The first man Adam became a living being (an individual personality); the last Adam (Christ) became life-giving Spirit [restoring the dead to life].AMP

2Cor 5:17   Therefore, if anyone is in Christ, he is a new creation; old things have passed away; behold, all things have become new.
I am a new creation
(You are a new species, no longer ordinary, My child; a new power source is flowing through you).

Eph 2:10   For we are His workmanship, created in Christ Jesus for good works, which God prepared beforehand that we should walk in them.
I am Your workmanship
(My work of art; every day as you respond to Me saying, 'Yes Lord', I transform you to become more and more beautiful).

1Cor 1:30-31 But of Him you are in Christ Jesus, who became for us wisdom from God—and righteousness and sanctification and redemption—that, as it is written, 'He who glories, let him glory in the Lord'.
I am in Christ
(Hidden in Me, part of Me, My body).

Col 1:27   To them God willed to make known what are the riches of the glory of this mystery among the Gentiles: which is Christ in you the hope of glory.
and **Christ lives in me**
(All that I am, the fullness of God, lives, throbs in you).

John 15:5   I am the vine, you are the branches. He who abides in Me, and I in him, bears much fruit; for without Me you can do nothing.

1Cor 6:17   But he who is joined to the Lord is one spirit with Him.

1Thes 5:17   pray without ceasing
I am one with you as a branch is of a vine; we commune always

(No more do you yearn to get into My Presence. You are there. We are one. There is no reason to leave My Presence. Let My life flow through you, and bear much fruit).

Is 54:17b "... And their righteousness is from Me, Says the LORD,"

Rom 5:17 For if by the one man's offence death reigned through the one, much more those who receive abundance of grace and of the gift of righteousness will reign in life through the One, Jesus Christ.
I have received the gift of Your righteousness
(My nature, not through anything you do, but because of My shed blood. It is a love gift. Now, you are in My Presence with no sense of condemnation or inferiority, and you have the same authority over the enemy which I exercised. We are as one. My nature is in you, so, for example, no more do you try to love; you can 'be' love).

Prov 28:1 The wicked flee when no one pursues, but the righteous are bold as a lion.
— **so I am as bold as a lion**
(Relying on Me within, you know no fear; expect only victory).

2Pet 1:3-4 ... His divine power has given to us all things that pertain to life and godliness, through the knowledge of Him who called us by glory and virtue, by which have been given to us exceedingly great and precious promises, that through these you may be partakers of the divine nature, having escaped the corruption that is in the world through lust.
I am a partaker of Your Divine nature
(My life, the Word is living in you, is you. Like Me, you do not fear, you do not get sick; it is not your nature).

John 8:12 Then Jesus spoke to them again, saying, "I am the light of the World. He who follows Me shall not walk in darkness, but have the light of life."

Matt 5:14 "You are the light of the world. A city that is set on a hill cannot be hidden."

I am the light of the world
(and light describes the created world!)

Rom 8:5-17   For you did not receive the spirit of bondage again to fear, but you received the Spirit of adoption by whom we cry out, 'Abba, Father'. The Spirit Himself bears witness with

our spirit that we are children of God, and if children, then heirs—heirs of God and joint heirs with Christ, ...
I am a son/daughter of the King of Kings
(A joint heir with Me, walk as royalty).

Phil 4:19   And my God shall supply all your need according to His riches in glory by Christ Jesus.
I know You will supply all my needs
(The whole world is Mine. Even in the natural a father tries to supply the needs of his children. Much more will I provide for you my beloved)

Is 43:7   "Everyone who is called by My name, whom I have created for My glory; I have formed him, yes, I have made him."
Is 60:1   Arise, shine; for your light has come! And the glory of the LORD is risen upon you.
I have been created to manifest Your glory
(I see you now, clothed in My glory, My Presence)

John 17:22   And the glory which You gave Me I have given them, that they may be one just as We are one;
Ps 97:5   The mountains melt like wax at the presence of the Lord, at the presence of the Lord of the whole earth.
2Cor 3:18   But we all, with unveiled face, beholding as in a mirror the glory of the Lord, are being transformed into the same image from glory to glory, just as by the Spirit of the Lord.
I have received Your glory
(So that we can be as one, as I was with My Father. You carry My awesome Presence. My glory is more powerful than any cultural bondage. Mountains melt like wax in the Presence of the Lord. As you focus on Me, I change you from glory to glory).

2Cor 1:21 Now He who establishes us with you in Christ and has anointed us is God,

1 John 2:27 But the anointing which you have received from Him abides in you, and you do not need that anyone teach you; but as the same anointing teaches you concerning all things, and is true, and is not a lie, and just as it has taught you, you will abide in Him.
**I am as anointed as You were when on earth
(Exactly the same source of super-natural power, the Holy Spirit, Who lived in Me is now in you. You can be as sensitive to My prompting as I was to My Father, and release whatever is required, as I did.)**

1Cor 2:16 'For who has known the mind of the Lord that he may instruct Him?' But we have the mind of Christ.
**I have Your mind, the mind of Christ
(Transformed by the living Word. That old mindset, self-centred, fearful and negative is becoming vibrant, positive and creative).**

1John 16:13 However, when He, the Spirit of truth, has come, He will guide you into all truth; for He will not speak on His own authority, but whatever He hears He will speak; and He will tell you things to come.

1Cor 2:12 Now we have received, not the spirit of the world, but the Spirit who is from God, that we might know the things that have been freely given to us by God.
**I am able to understand the Truth and mysteries
(Delight in the truth, be so expectant and I will reveal My heart to you).**

John 10:27 My sheep hear My voice, and I know them, and they follow Me.
**I hear Your voice
(Expect Me to guide, prompt, even speak to you twenty four hours a day, whatever you are doing).**

My True Identity

Is 12:2-3	Behold, God is my salvation, I will trust and not be afraid; 'For Yah, the Lord, is my strength and song; He also has become my salvation.' Therefore with joy you will draw water from the wells of salvation.
John 4:14	... But the water that I shall give him will become in him a fountain of water springing up into everlasting life.
John 7:38	He who believes in Me, as the Scripture has said, out of his heart will flow rivers of living water.

I draw water with joy from the well of salvation within

(All of Me, My love, joy, peace, wisdom, power, healing, forgiveness etc, is within you. Continually draw from it with joy, with confidence, and release it).

Luke 17:21	"nor will they say, 'See here!' or 'See there!' For indeed, the kingdom of God is within you."

I have Your kingdom within

(All you ever want or need is within you. See as I do, My glory in all things, everyone saved, healed, rejoicing.)

Rom 12:3	For I say, through the grace given to me, to everyone who is among you, not to think of himself more highly than he ought to think, but to think soberly, as God has dealt to each one a measure of faith.
Rom 1:17	For in it (the gospel) the righteousness of God is revealed from faith to faith; as it is written, 'The just shall live by faith'.

I have Your faith within

(a Divinely implanted measure of faith—use it so that it grows from faith to faith)

1Cor 1:30	But of Him you are in Christ Jesus, who became for us wisdom from God—and righteousness and sanctification and redemption—

I have Your wisdom within

(Expect it to flow when you draw it up from the well within).

Rom 5:5   Now hope does not disappoint, because the love of God has been poured out in our hearts by the Holy Spirit who was given to us.
I have Your love within
(Including My zeal. It compels you be that chosen vessel through whom My glorious purposes are realized. I implore you to release it to bless this hungry desolate world).

John 14:27   Peace I leave with you, My peace I give to you; not as the world gives do I give to you. Let not your heart be troubled, neither let it be afraid.
I have Your peace within
(Such confidence in Me, wholeness, rest).

John 15:11   These things I have spoken to you, that My joy may remain in you, and that your joy may be full.

Neh 8:10   .... Do not sorrow, for the joy of the Lord is your strength.
I have Your joy within
(The fruit of being one with Me as two lovers and it is your strength in any circumstance).

Prov 29:18   Where there is no revelation (prophetic vision), the people cast off restraint; but happy is he who keeps the law.
I have a vision
(Let it be a driving force, to walk just as I walked, with all the supernatural gifts flowing. Seek Me re your individual vision and then ardently pursue it. Keep it burning, do not let the enemy quench it).

5

AUTHORITY

Few Christians realize, know inside the truth that the enemy has been totally defeated. He has no power over us other than what we give him. He is excellent at deceiving, but if we refuse to receive his lies and keep the door closed, he is no problem. We know his strategies. He tries to get our focus off God and onto ourselves, (as he did in the garden of Eden). Then he encourages us to rebel against God, to do things our way, independently of Him. Another ploy is to get us to fear, indeed to have more faith in the negative reports which he instigates rather than in the truth, the Word of God. It is so important for our mindset to change from being a victim of circumstances to being able to change those circumstances, to rise up, take responsibility and dominion and to rule (Rom 5:17).

We need to speak aggressively to the enemy when he attacks, so that he knows we will tolerate no nonsense. When in India and Zambia I taught the Christians, some of whom had just given their lives to God, to use this authority. I taught them to use it to make sure the enemy could have no place in their lives. They would loudly, aggressively declare, 'In Jesus Name—go!', with the same ruthlessness they would use if a dog or a goat had come into their house. When they did this the enemy ran from them terrified. They applied this to the spirit of poverty which is so much part of their culture. Then they would speak in the truth, that 'I am rich'. I taught them how to stand on the blessings of Abraham, which declare that whatever they put their hand to will prosper etc: They knew they were free. They also used their authority to rebuke any sickness; to command it to leave them and to speak in the truth that they are healed. Many, at one meeting about 40% of them, wanted to testify to distinct changes in their bodies. What was so exciting for me was the testimonies that followed. For example, an elderly woman shared the following week, how her grandchild had been very ill, and how she had laid hands on her and told the sickness to go. Immediately the child asked for food! God wants every born-again believer to walk in the authority He has purchased for us. By so doing we reveal Jesus and the glorious life of freedom He has purchased for us. Our lives and speech must not just be in words, but in the demonstration of His power. Our lives will attract others to our Lord. God intends this to be the natural life of a 'butterfly' or a new creation.

Declarations

Col 2:15 Having disarmed principalities and powers He made a public spectacle of them, triumphing over them in it.

Rev 1:18 I am He who lives, and was dead, and behold, I am alive forever, Amen. And I have the keys of Hades and of Death.
I know You have defeated the enemy; You triumphed over him
(Now you are in Me, so make the decision never to be defeated by him).

Matt 28:18 And Jesus came and spoke to them, saying, 'All authority has been given to Me in heaven and on earth'.

Eph 1:20-21 ... He raised Him(Jesus)from the dead and seated Him at His right hand in the heavenly places, far above all principality and power and might and dominion, and every name that is named, not only in this age but also in that which is to come.

Eph 2:6 ... and raised us up together, and made us sit together in the heavenly places in Christ Jesus.
I am seated together with You in heavenly places at the Father's right hand, the place of authority
(You died with Me, were buried with Me and rose together with Me with the same resurrection life. It is a spiritual law that a lower authority always has to bow to a higher one. When on earth I demonstrated this authority over the enemy and nature. You have this same authority).

My True Identity

Luke 10:19   Behold I give **you** the authority to trample on serpents and scorpions, and over all the power of the enemy, and nothing shall by any means hurt you.
I have been given this authority to trample on serpents and scorpions and over all the power of the enemy.
(re all aspects of the curse—sickness, depression, fear etc: Walk in this authority purchased for you. the enemy is under your feet. Whatever form he tries to take, decide he will become as dust. Do not just be defensive. What are you going to tread on today?)

Acts 1:8   But you shall receive power (ability, efficiency, and might) when the Holy Spirit has come upon you, and you shall be My witnesses in Jerusalem and all Judea and Samaria and to the ends (the very bounds) of the earth." AMP

Eph 1:19:20   ... what is the immeasurable and unlimited and surpassing greatness of His power in and for us who believe, as demonstrated in the working of His mighty strength, which He exerted in Christ when He raised Him from the dead and seated Him at His [own] right hand in the heavenly [places]. AMP
I have the mighty power of God within me
(There is no limit to what you can do, transforming darkness into light and so revealing Me—My Presence, My love, My glory!)

James 4:7   Therefore submit to God. Resist the devil and he will flee from you.
I resist the devil and he has to flee
(He is as terrified of you as he was of Me when you stand in and use that authority).

Phil 2:9-10   Therefore God also has highly exalted Him and given Him the name which is above every name, that at the name of Jesus every knee should bow, of those in heaven, and of those on earth, and of those under the earth,
I use the name of Jesus knowing every knee must bow to the King of Kings
(—it is as if I am speaking).

Mark 11:23	For assuredly, I say to you, whoever says to this mountain, 'Be removed and be cast into the sea,' and does not doubt in his heart, but believes that those things he says will be done, he will have whatever he says.
Matt 17:20	... if you have faith as a mustard seed, you will say to this mountain, 'Move from here to there,' and it will move; and nothing will be impossible for you.

I speak to mountains (problems) **and they are removed**
(Know the authority in your mouth; nothing is impossible for you).

2Cor 10:4-5	For the weapons of our warfare are not carnal but mighty in God for pulling down strongholds, casting down arguments and every high thing that exalts itself against the knowledge of God, bringing every thought into captivity to the obedience of Christ,

I demolish strongholds, old mindsets
('You' trying, good works, pride, etc. Imagine dynamite placed under the wall and see it explode).

1John 5:4	For whatever is born of God overcomes the world. And this is the victory that has overcome the world—our faith.
2Cor 2:14	Now thanks be to God who always leads us in triumph in Christ, and through us diffuses the fragrance of His knowledge in every place.
Heb 3:6	... And it is we who are [now members] of this house, if we hold fast and firm to the end our joyful and exultant confidence and sense of triumph in our hope [in Christ]. AMP

I am an over-comer; victory is certain—with joy I hold fast to Your word
(Fight the fight of faith, refuse to accept defeat).

Rom 8:37	Yet in all these things we are more than conquerors through Him who loved us.

I am more than a conqueror
(Not just a conqueror; the issue is what to do with the spoils).

Josh 1:3	Every place that the sole of your foot will tread upon I have given you . . . .
	Every place that the sole of my foot will tread upon will be possessed for You
	(Expect that wherever I take you, darkness will be destroyed, and My light, My glory released).
Num 14:9	"Only do not rebel against the Lord, nor fear the people of the land, for they are our bread; their protection has departed from them, and the Lord is with us. Do not fear them."
2Cor 3:18	But we all with unveiled face, beholding as in a mirror the glory of the Lord, are being transformed into the same image from glory to glory, just as by the Spirit of the Lord.
	The enemy is as bread to me
	(What are you going to eat today My beloved? And thereby grow strong through victory after victory).
Rev 1:6	and has made us kings and priests to His God and Father, to Him be glory and dominion forever and ever. Amen.
Ecc 8:4	Where the word of a king is, there is power; and who may say to him, "What are you doing?"
	I have been made a king
	(It has already been done!)
Rom 5:17	For if by one man's offence death reigned through the one, much more those who receive abundance of grace and of the gift of righteousness will reign in life through the One, Jesus Christ.
Matt 10:8	Heal the sick, cleanse the lepers, raise the dead, cast out demons. Freely you have received, freely give.
	I reign as a king in life
	(Rule, speak to your body, relationships and circumstances, destroy the works of the enemy, release the kingdom of God).
Mark 11:22	So Jesus answered and said to them, 'Have faith in God,' (in Greek, 'Have the God kind of faith')
Rom 4:17	. . . . God who gives life to the dead and calls those things which do not exist as though they did:

I call things which do not exist as though they did. (This is the creative power of your words).

Eph 6:11 Put on the whole armour of God, that you may be able to stand against the wiles of the devil.
I wear and use the armour of God (Stand in the fullness of what I have given you and refuse to be moved).

Deut 28:13 And the Lord will make you the head and not the tail; you shall be above only, and not be beneath, if you heed the commandments of the Lord your God . . . .

1John 4:4 You are of God, little children, and have overcome them, because He who is in you is greater than he who is in the world.
I am the head and not the tail (The strongest spirit dominates, and greater is He that is in you, than he that is in the world. Do not tolerate any work of the enemy).

Eph 4:26-27 'Be angry, and do not sin': do not let the sun go down on your wrath, nor give place to the devil.

Rom 12:9 Let love be without hypocrisy. Abhor what is evil. Cling to what is good.
I am angry at what the enemy has done, hate what is evil, and refuse to be lulled to sleep and compromise (Let My love in you stir up righteous anger instilling a passion to release those in bondage).

James 1:2-4 My brethren, count it all joy when you fall into various trials, knowing that the testing of your faith produces patience. But let patience have its perfect work, that you may be perfect and complete, lacking nothing.

Acts 4:29-30 'Now, Lord, look on their threats, and grant to Your servants that with all boldness they may speak Your word, by stretching out Your hand to heal and that signs and wonders may be done through the name of Your holy Servant Jesus'.
I see trials as new challenges, and rejoice in them (You know I will intervene gloriously).

Phil 4:4	Rejoice in the Lord always. Again I will say, rejoice!
Hab 3:17-18	Though . . . . Yet I will rejoice in the LORD, I will joy in The God of my salvation.
Rom 14:17	for the kingdom of God is not eating and drinking, but righteousness and peace and joy in the Holy Spirit.

**I rejoice always
(knowing that trials are stepping stones to new victories)**

6

WALK

Our walk is an expression of who we are. Our lives should be an epistle, or an illustration of the Word of God; the Word now living in our flesh. No more do we try to love or be victorious, as we did when we were 'caterpillars'. It is the nature of a 'butterfly' to love and to be victorious. We are love, are over-comers. The scriptures say it, we believe, receive it and live it. If insufficient love seems to be flowing, we do not ask for more as all His love is within. No, we ask for more to be released. If we have suffered defeat, we now realize that victory is our inheritance, and refuse to accept defeat any more. God's people are destroyed not through the enemy but through lack of knowledge. Now we know, so we can simply ask forgiveness for accepting the lies of the enemy in any area, and decide in our hearts never again to listen to those lies but to accept only victory. Then we start applying the Word; start speaking out the desired outcome, receiving it, thanking God for it, becoming pregnant with it. This is putting the Word to work.

I have found that **this can be applied to our emotions too**. When we lived as 'caterpillars', so much of our energy was wasted. It leaked away in worry, fear, etc. As our minds are renewed we discover we are commanded not to worry (Matt 6:25); butterflies are free from it. In the same way we have brought our minds into the captivity of Christ, to think only as the Word describes, we can do the same with our emotions, so that our emotional energy is not leaked away. Our heart, our desires, motives, are of key importance to God. 'Keep your heart with all diligence, for out of it spring the issues of life' (Prov 4:23).

We are commanded to love Him with all of our heart and love others with the same love. Our whole life can be an expression of such a heart, all we do and think. I have found that by surrendering any other emotions, fear, worry, lust, we can walk free of them, standing in victory in those areas. A beautiful fruit of doing this is having so much more energy. It is not wasted. It is being used as the God who made us intended it to be used, loving Him with all our hearts and others with the same love. Some people feel they do not want to give up their 'pleasure on-the-side', their addiction is sweet—so the enemy has persuaded them. Once they see the glorious freedom, the fullness of joy which is their portion, as they live their lives as God intended, the deception of the enemy has no more weight. 'Butterflies' live an abundant life in every area, not hidden, but visible for all to see, Hallelujah! I believe when those in the world see the fire of His love, His life burning in us, they will not be able to resist Him. 'The whole earth is eagerly waiting for the revealing of the sons of God' (Rom 8:19).

Declarations

Deut 6:5   You shall love the Lord your God with all your heart, with all your soul, and with all your strength.

Matt 22:37   Jesus said to him, 'You shall love the Lord your God with all your heart, with all your soul, and with all your mind'.
I love You with all my heart, all my soul and all my strength
(nothing left over).

1Pet 1:8, 9   Whom having not seen you love. Though now you do not see Him, yet believing, you rejoice with joy inexpressible and full of glory, receiving the end of your faith—the salvation of your souls.
I love You so I am filled with an inexpressible, triumphant and heavenly joy
(Involves your mind, will, emotions, body so this is total salvation, nothing left out—I love it).

Rom 5:5   Now hope does not disappoint, because the love of God has been poured out in our hearts by the Holy Spirit who was given to us.

Eph 3:19   to know the love of Christ which passes knowledge; that you may be filled with all the fullness of God.

I am getting to know Your love for me and experiencing being filled with all Your fullness
(If not living in My fullness, there is more to know . . . .).

Ps 40:8 'I delight to do Your will, o my God, and Your law is within my heart'.
I delight to do Your will,
1Thes 5:16 Rejoice always.
—rejoicing always

Jer 31:33 But this is the covenant that I will make with the house of Israel after those days, says the Lord: I will put My law in their minds, and write it on their hearts; and I will be their God, and they shall be My people.
Rom 8:2 For the law of the Spirit of life in Christ Jesus has made me free from the law of sin and death.
Phil 2:12-13 . . . work out your own salvation with fear and trembling; for it is God who works in you both to will and to do for His good pleasure.
I delight in Your laws that are in my heart.
(They are part of you and work in you, motivate you to love and to walk as I did when on earth)—hallelujah!

Matt 22:39 And the second (great commandment) is like it; 'You shall love your neighbour as yourself'.
I love others with the same (passionate) **love,**
Matt 6:15 But if you do not forgive men their trespasses, neither will your Father forgive your trespasses.
—and am quick to forgive
(to restore love).

1John 4:4 You are of God, little children, and have overcome them, because He who is in you is greater than he who is in the world.
I walk in the power of Your love
(My love in you is greater, above the self-centeredness in the world).

Rom 12:11	Never lag in zeal and in earnest endeavor; be aglow and burning with the Spirit, serving the Lord. AMP **I am aglow, burning in the spirit serving You** **(With joy and zeal).**
Heb 12:29	For our God is a consuming fire.
Ps 104:4	Who makes His angels spirits, His ministers a flame of fire.
Luke 12:49	"I came to send fire on the earth, and how I wish it were already kindled!" **I am a flame of fire** **(truly alive)**
Matt 5:8	Blessed are the pure in heart, for they shall see God.
Prov 4:23	Keep your heart with all diligence, for out of it spring the issues of life. **I keep my heart with all diligence** **(Not to grieve Me; no trace of pride or self-thoughts).**
Gal 5:16	I say then: Walk in the Spirit, and you shall not fulfil the lust of the flesh. **I walk in the Spirit,**
Rom 8:14	For as many as are led by the Spirit of God, these are sons of God. **—am led by the Spirit**
Eph 5:18	And do not be drunk with wine, in which is dissipation; but be filled with the Spirit, **—and filled with the Spirit** **(In harmony with Me, 100% submitted; always expectant of Me).**
2Cor 4:18	while we do not look at the things which are seen, but at the things which are not seen. For the things which are seen are temporary, but the things which are not seen are eternal.
Rom 8:5-6	For those who live according to the flesh set their minds on the things of the flesh, but those who live according to the Spirit, the things of the Spirit. For to be carnally minded is death, but to be spiritually minded is life and peace. **I focus on things unseen; my mind is set on things of the Spirit** **(My glorious purposes. The effect is life and peace).**

1Sam 16:7   But the Lord said to Samuel, 'Do not look at his appearance or at his physical stature, because I have refused him. For the Lord does not see as man sees; for man looks at the outward appearance, but the Lord looks at the heart.

2Cor 5:16   Therefore, from now on, we regard no one according to the flesh. Even though we have known Christ according to the flesh, yet now we know Him thus no longer.
I do not respond to the appearance of others, but their hearts
(their relationship with Me and how to encourage them).

John 4:24   God is Spirit, and those who worship Him must worship in spirit and truth'.
I worship in spirit and truth
(Draw with joy from the spirit within. It is the love language of your heart: it can be expressed in so many ways. With all your heart soul and body embrace Me and the Word, so there is harmony in you, no hypocrisy. It will be as an open heaven; like an electric circuit open to the source of your life).

1 Thes 5:17   pray without ceasing
    — praying always
(Switched on continually, whatever you are doing).

Phil 4:13   I can do all things through Christ who strengthens me.
I know that I can do all things You ask of me through the anointing within
(No limit — All of My glorious power will flow as required).

Prov 3:5   Trust in the Lord with all your heart, and lean not on your own understanding;
I trust You with all my heart
(You rely on Me, you know I am faithful).

John 1:1, 14   In the beginning was the Word, and the Word was with God, and the Word was God. And the Word became flesh and dwelt among us, and we beheld His glory, the glory as of the only begotten of the Father, full of grace and truth.

	I trust the Word, the Truth, as You are the living Word (rest your weight on it).
Is 66:2	But on this one will I look; on him who is poor and of a contrite spirit, and who trembles at My word'. **I tremble at Your word** **(your heart saying, 'Yes Lord'. It reveals My awesome glorious power—receive it by faith and do it).**
Jer 15:16	Your words were found, and I ate them, and Your word was to me the joy and rejoicing of my heart; **I feast on the Word; it is the joy and rejoicing of my heart** **(Embrace it, eat it, and digest it, so that it ignites within).**
Heb 4:12	For the word of God is living and powerful, and sharper than any two-edged sword, piercing even to the division of soul and spirit, and of joints and marrow, and is a discerner of the thoughts and intents of the heart. **—it is living and powerful, sharper than any two-edged sword** **(It penetrates the depths of your heart, able to change you, release you—Glory to God!).**
Jer 23:29	"Is not My word like a fire?" says the LORD, "And like a hammer that breaks the rock in pieces?"
Jer 20:9b	. . . But His word was in my heart like a burning fire shut up in my bones; I was weary of holding it back, and I could not. **—it is burning within** **(Divine energy)**
1Thes 2:13	. . . the word of God which you heard from us, you welcomed it not as the word of men, but as it is in truth, the word of God, which also effectively works in you who believe. **—it is working effectively in me** **(Expect miracles daily).**

Acts 19:20 So the word of the Lord grew mightily and prevailed.
—it is prevailing
(lives and situations are changing).

Rom 4:20-21 He did not waver at the promise of God through unbelief, but was strengthened in faith, giving glory to God, and being fully convinced that what He had promised He was also able to perform.
I do not stagger at Your promise but embrace it with joy
(Know that I long for you to receive it. This is the fight of faith, through which you will grow strong).

Dan 11:32b ". . . the people who know their God shall be strong, and carry out great exploits.
2Chron 16:9 "For the eyes of the LORD run to and fro throughout the whole earth, to show Himself strong on behalf of those whose heart is loyal to Him . . . .
Mark 11:24 Therefore I say to you, whatever things you ask when you pray, believe that you receive them, and you will have them.
I pray, speak out the word and receive it now
(Even if not evident, possess it, be pregnant with it; declare it done, give thanks for it).

Prov 18:21 Death and life are in the power of the tongue, and those who love it will eat its fruit.
I know life and death are in the power of my tongue
(Only speak out good positive words, and they will come into being. Never speak negatively).

1Thes 5:18 in everything give thanks; for this is the will of God in Christ Jesus for you.
I give thanks in everything
(For My Presence with you, and in trials for the outcome which you speak into being).

2Cor 5:7 For we walk by faith, not by sight,
Heb 11:6 But without faith it is impossible to please Him, for he who comes to God must believe that He is, and that He is a rewarder of those who diligently seek Him.

1Pet 1:7 . . . the genuineness of your faith, being much more precious than gold that perishes, though it is tested by fire, may be found to praise, honor, and glory at the revelation of Jesus Christ,
I walk by faith, not by sight
(Stand on the promise, not affected by circumstances or feelings).

Heb 4:3, 10 For we who have believed do enter that rest, ... For he who has entered His rest has himself also ceased from his works as God did from His.
I believe, so I have entered Your rest and ceased from struggling
(Now, your confidence is in Me; you rely on Me, on the Word. Your life is becoming a manifestation of the Word).

Gal 6:14 But God forbid that I should boast except in the cross of our Lord Jesus Christ, by whom the world has been crucified to me, and I to the world.
I glory, even boast in the power of the cross and the power of Your blood
(Look at what I and your Father have done for you—the glorious abundant life now yours).

John 15:5 I am the vine, you are the branches. He who abides in Me, and I in him, bears much fruit; for without Me you can do nothing.
I abide in You, Your Word, so I produce much fruit (fruit that remains).

1John 2:6 He who says he abides in Him ought himself also to walk just as He walked.
—and walk just as You did,

Mk 16:17,18 And these signs will follow those who believe; In My name they will cast out demons; they will speak with new tongues; they will take up serpents; and if they drink anything deadly, it will by no means hurt them; they will lay hands on the sick, and they will recover.
—casting out demons,

(The Spirit in you is greater than he in the world and must bow to My Word).
>   —laying hands on the sick and seeing them recover

(through touch, releasing My Spirit to evict the spirit that sustains the sickness).

John 7:38	'He who believes in Me, as the Scripture has said, out of his heart will flow rivers of living water.'
Is 11:2-3	The Spirit of the Lord shall rest upon Him, the Spirit of wisdom and understanding, the Spirit of counsel and might, the Spirit of knowledge and of the fear of the Lord. His delight is in the fear of the Lord . . .

I release continually rivers of living water
(drawing from the well of salvation, the fullness of Your spirit and Your life).

Ezek 47:9	And it shall be that every living thing that moves, wherever the rivers go, will live. There will be a very great multitude of fish, because these waters go there; for they will be healed, and everything will live wherever the river goes.

>   **—bringing life wherever I go**

(My love flowing from you, melting hearts, and just as I did opening eyes, releasing captives).

7

PURPOSE

What freedom it is that the focus of my life is not what I make of it, but that God, Almighty God will use it to the full with His resources. It is not important what other people think of me, so I am not controlled by them. I am not trying to become someone in my own strength, always evaluating and finding that I fail or come short of what I desire. No, no, I long for others to know, to walk in His glorious light, freedom. Each one of us has their own particular calling or area where there is a distinctive anointing. We know that it can only be realized through the very life of God throbbing, flowing through us and it will bear glorious fruit. So with joy we delight to do what He asks of us, knowing He will intervene . . . . What a life!

I have found that a beautiful outcome of my heart being united with my Lord's, is to discover that so many brothers and sisters throughout the world have the same heart. Factors which normally divide are irrelevant. What joy it is to find that I am one with an Indian or African, irrespective of the fact that for so many of them, food on the table next day is uncertain or that nine of them live in one room. Glory to God! I praise and thank Him that once they have heard the truth, they are discovering for themselves the blessings of Abraham which are theirs. Their situations are changing. There is a new joy in their hearts. They are stepping into the inheritance God longs for every believer to possess. The river of God is flowing from them and they are becoming blessings to others—Hallelujah!

Declarations

Exod 19:5-6 Now therefore, if you will indeed obey My voice and keep My covenant, then you shall be a special treasure to Me above all people; for all the earth is Mine, and you shall be to Me a kingdom of priests and a holy nation' . . .

1Pet 2:9 But you are a chosen generation, a royal priesthood, a holy nation, His own special people, that you may proclaim the praises of Him who called you out of darkness into His marvellous light;
For You to be glorified
(In everything you think, speak and do—open heaven).

Matt 6:10 Your kingdom come. Your will be done on earth as it is in heaven.
To establish Your kingdom on earth
(All knowing Me, the Word, and living it).

1John 3:8 . . . For this purpose the Son of God was manifested, that He might destroy the works of the devil.
To destroy the works of the enemy
(That have tied up so many).

Luke 4:18 The Spirit of the Lord is upon Me, because He has anointed Me to preach the gospel to the poor; He has sent Me to heal the brokenhearted, to proclaim liberty to the captives and recovery of sight to the blind, to set at liberty those who are oppressed;

Mark 16:20 And they went out and preached everywhere, the Lord working with them and confirming the word through the accompanying signs. Amen.
To preach the gospel
(expecting miracles to confirm the Word),
To release captives, open blind eyes and heal the broken hearted
(Expect Divine encounters).

John 17:18   Just as You sent Me into the world, I also have sent them into the world). AMP
To walk as You did when on earth, revealing Your glory
(Walking on water, with no props—manifesting the same God given love and authority; doing the same glorious things).

8

HOW TO LIVE A SCRIPTURE

The Word of God is BRILLIANT

It is glorious to have the **Living word** inside us, to know the truth of the Word deep within. Then when we speak the Word, the situation is changed, the person is healed, we find the job, relationships are restored etc:

> **'Is not My word like a fire?'** says the Lord, **'and like a hammer that breaks in pieces the rock (of most stubborn resistance)?'** Jer 23:29. AMP

What joy it is to step into the Word, to possess it, to live it. In Luke 4:21 Jesus announced that **'Today this Scripture is fulfilled in your hearing'**. Jesus stepped into that scripture. In other words, He said 'This Scripture describes Me'. We can similarly make any scripture our possession; especially those describing who we are as new creations or ones that have particularly touched our heart.

I have made use of the word **'BRILLIANT'** to help us to digest a specific scripture and live it out. The **Word** is **brilliant** in what it can do in and through us. The consonants in **'BRILLIANT'** can be used to provide a structure for this.

BELIEVE	Know it is the living Word, spoken by Almighty God
RECEIVE	Possess it personally with joy
LIVE IT evident in	**L**anguage—speak it out
LIVE IT evident in	**L**ifestyle—changing the way you behave
NOW	Today release it, use it
TRIUMPHANTLY	Know it works.

How does it work?

Take a particular scripture, one that has spoken to you, or perhaps one of the Declarations in "My True Identity". Then use it as follows;

BELIEVE   Know it is the living Word, spoken by Almighty God. Tremble at His word. Thank Him for the truth.
Believe as a child believes.
Lay aside the old negative thinking of the world.
Let Him speak to you as if He is in the room with you.

RECEIVE   Possess it with **Joy** personally, with a **thankful heart**.
Put your name in the scripture.
Again give no place to your old way of thinking.
Receive it deep inside with such joy.
Delight in it — meditate on it.
Speak it out often, softly, loudly.
Know as you do, as you say the same as the Scriptures, you will become more and more confident and excited about it.
A young child given a strange present, may look at it from different angles, touch it, explore it. All his attention is focused on it, so he gets to know it, even before using it.
You can similarly explore and delight in the truth.
Use your mind to the full; what does this word mean?
Are there any other similar scriptures?
The Holy Spirit Who lives in you will help to reveal the glory of the truth.

LIVE IT evident in my   **Language** —
Decide, I will delight in speaking out this truth, sharing it with others its beauty, excitement ...

LIVE IT evident in my   **Lifestyle** —
Decide to put it to work. I will no longer react as I always have done. I now **know** the truth so there will be **victory** in this area.

NOW   **Today** my life will be different. Think of specific times or places, or issues, which will not be the same—Hallelujah!

TRIUMPHANTLY   Know it will happen.
Be so **expectant** that the Holy Spirit, who is living in you, will move mightily in you to see that it happens—that it will be a reality today.

Example 1

There is no fear in love; but perfect love casts out fear, because Fear involves torment. he who fears has not been made perfect in love (1John 4:18).

I am loved perfectly

Believe

It is so glorious, that I am loved perfectly by Almighty God. As I get to **know** this truth **inside**, I will be free of fear, of people, circumstances etc:—praise God!

The Scriptures show His love. It is there throughout the Old Testament. His people rebelled again and again, but God longed for them to return to Him so He could bless them. **'I will heal their backsliding, I will love them freely, for my anger has turned away from him (Israel)'** (Hos14:4). This perfect love is shown in the Gospels. How He sent His precious Son to die, so that all of us who have gone our own way could know Him, and receive the extraordinary inheritance He has won for us. Almighty God had, and always has had, wonderful plans for His own children. That means for me. These plans can only be mine if I believe and respond to this beautiful love. **I will believe it!**

Thank You Lord for this truth. It is the **living word of Almighty God**. I tremble at Your Word; I dare not disagree with any part of it. I will give no place to my old 'caterpillar' mind, full of negatives, and fear. I will believe Your truth as a child believes—and trusts. I will believe it as if You were standing in the room speaking to me—Thank You Lord.

Receive

With **joy** and such a thankful heart I receive this love. I believe what Your Word says, that **God Almighty loves me (my name)**, that **I am so precious to him**. Thank You Lord. Let joy rise up from within. What peace and confidence it gives me.

I will delight in Your love and think much about what it means for me. I am loved perfectly. I will speak it often, softly—whisper it so it sinks deep into my heart. You are with me always, I can never be alone. Nothing can separate me from Your love. I have been through tough times, but You were with me, You brought me through. You know every detail about my life, my strengths and weaknesses, successes and failures, and yet You still love me. Even more glorious is that You want to bless me. I will speak it loudly, declaring it, or even sing it—You have glorious plans for me—wow!

How can I fear when I know You love me perfectly and You are with me always? I will totally trust in this glorious truth.

Live it—Language

I will not keep to myself how wonderful it is to know that I am loved by You. I may even sing about You—not just when alone! I will encourage others to know this beautiful love for themselves—Hallelujah

Live it—Lifestyle

I will not hide this joy in my heart. I will have a new twinkle in my eye.

I will be ready to share about why I have this inner joy and confidence with anyone I meet.

I have been frightened of my (husband, boss, child, work etc:) but not now. When I see them there will be such peace in my heart, such confidence in You.

I will be able to love them with Your love. I know You will give me the words to say—praise God!

Now

Today I will be different, when by myself, on the way to work, while working, in the shops, wherever I am there will be a new joy in my heart. I refuse to fear . . . . Instead I expect You to protect me, to give me wisdom or whatever I need.

Triumphantly

I know it will work. I am so expectant. I know others will see a difference in me and be drawn to You as a result—praise God! I will no longer be the victim, but will shine with Your love, Your life. The situation will be changed—glory to God!

Example 2

Behold, I give you the authority to trample on serpents and scorpions, and over all the power of the enemy, and nothing shall by any means hurt you (Luke 10:19).

I have been given authority to trample on serpents and scorpions and over all the power of the enemy

Believe

When Jesus was on earth, people were amazed at the authority with which He spoke. All authority had been given to Him, and He used it over the enemy, casting out demons, healing the sick, stilling the storm etc: On the cross Jesus defeated the enemy for us. He triumphed over him—glory to God! He has given this same authority to us. I give you authority—over **all** the power of the enemy. The enemy is the author of all aspects of the curse, fear, sickness, depression poverty etc: We have been given authority to trample on, and to destroy any evidence of them in our lives, and in the lives of those around us. To do this He has given us His Name, so that when we speak it, it is as if Jesus was speaking. Also we are told that if we resist the enemy, as we rebuke him, he has to flee, or run in terror (James 4:7)—glory to God. As we stand in these glorious truths, nothing can possibly harm us. This is Your Word. This is the truth. I will believe it.

Receive

Thank You Lord, that You have given me (my name) this authority. I will meditate on these glorious truths until I know them deep within. I will speak them out often; 'The same authority that You walked in,

I walk in. It is over all the power of the enemy. You have given it to me **to use**, to put to work'. In the Old Testament Your people had to plead for You to take action, for You to remove the problem. Now it is my responsibility. You ask me to speak to the problem with a prayer of faith, not doubting in my heart, and know that it has to move (Mark 11;23). Thank You Lord that nothing of the curse is greater than Your name. If sickness arises, I can rebuke it, 'In the Name of Jesus go', and it has to go. Then I declare, 'I am healed'. If fear tries to fill my heart, I can speak out, 'I refuse to fear ', and declare the truth, eg: 'Thank You Lord I have not a spirit of fear but of power, and of love and of a sound mind' (2Tim 1:7). 'Thank You Lord that You have made me free, so I am free—hallelujah!' I will use this authority in whatever form or place I see the enemy active. I declare 'victory over all the devices of the enemy'. For myself, 'I will tolerate no area of bondage, no sickness, no depression. I will receive no negative thoughts about myself.

I refuse to give place to any unbelief. I refuse to fear, I refuse to be sick—hallelujah! I thank You Lord that I am more than a conqueror—greater is He that is in me than he that is in the world—that You always lead me in triumph—praise Your glorious Name!

Live it—Language

I will seek opportunities to tell others about these truths. My language will have no negatives. I will speak of victory and encourage others to see it. More than that God wants every believer to use this authority He has given us so that they too can **walk in the reality** of the freedom He purchased for us, the abundant life, free of all the oppression and bondage of the enemy—glory to God!

Live it—Lifestyle

There is a particular area in my life where I need victory today (name it).

I declare to you, enemy, that you are going to be ground into the earth as dust. There will be 100% victory in this area. I will be so full of expectation. Others will see my confidence in You, Lord, and that it works, that it impacts everyday life. They will be drawn to You. What joy it will be to come alongside others going through the same problem and encourage them.

Now

Today, I have received a trickle of unbelief in (name the area). Forgive me Lord. If it arises again, I will aggressively rebuke it in Jesus Name, and speak out the truth—what You have specifically said, or promised in Your Word—with such joyful confidence (Heb 3:6b). In fact, if such thoughts arise, I will take it as a prompt to elaborate more on the desired result. I know You will reveal more. I am excited already. The enemy will be sorry he tried to implant such thoughts—glory to God!

Triumphantly

I am so full of **expectation**; victory will be my song—hallelujah. There will be many testimonies as the result of today—glory to God!

Example 3

For this reason we also thank God without ceasing, because when you received the word of God which you heard from us, you welcomed it not as the word of men, but as it is in truth, the word of God, which also effectively works in you who believe. (1Thes 2:13).

The Word of God is working effectively in me

Believe

It is the Spirit who gives life: the flesh profits nothing. The words that I speak to you are spirit and they are life (John 6:63). The Word of God received by a rational, carnal mind is of no value, but received by the Spirit of God in us, becomes life in us and through us—wow! For the word of God is living and powerful, and sharper than any two-edged sword, piercing even to the division of soul and spirit, and of joints and marrow, and is a discerner of the thoughts and intents of the heart (Heb 4:12). God wants His Word **to live in us** so that it works effectively. In the Greek the word effective is 'energeo' from which energy derives. It means 'the active operation or **working of power** and its **effectual results'**. In the early church, the Word was not just spoken, but demonstrated. Transformed lives, signs and wonders were its fruit. In Acts19:20 the scripture says, the **Word of the Lord grew mightily and prevailed**. The Word grew—praise God. It is living. Living things have their own dynamic and grow. The word 'prevailed' has the meaning of manifested power in reigning authority — hallelujah!

God wants the living Word to be released, manifested in and through the lives of each one of us, so revealing His glory. The Word has a mighty active ingredient. If someone takes a pill, it is only the active ingredient that is effective.

How can we let loose the active ingredient inherent in the Word? We are told to meditate on the word, and this has glorious results (Joshua 1:8). It was effective under the Old covenant, much more so now that the Spirit has been released. Col 3:16 tells us to, 'Let the word of Christ dwell in you richly in all wisdom, teaching and admonishing one another in psalms and hymns and spiritual songs, singing with grace in your hearts to the Lord'.

There are many non-verbal ways we can employ as well. Letting our bodies respond, like raising our hands in worship or dancing like David did, will enhance its meaning for us.

We are told to pray in the spirit, speaking in tongues. This will edify us, build ourselves up (Jude 20), and help us to know the **mysteries** of the living Word (1Cor 14:2).

Lord, I believe that as I do these things my spirit will be ignited with the very power, the inherent energy of the Word—hallelujah!

Receive

Thank You Lord, that I am a Spirit-filled, born again believer. Thank You that You have made my spirit to receive the living Word of God, so that it can become a living reality, expressed through my life—hallelujah! Yes, I will meditate on your Word, I will possess Your Word, incubate Your Word, and receive it, but not only through my mind . . .

When I receive a beautiful present from a friend, I may just say, 'thank you', but deep within I am at the same time rejoicing and longing to express love to that person. I may even express that rejoicing with a jump of joy, a wow! My whole being is involved. Such expressions increase the value, the meaning of that present to me, and my relationship with the person who gave it. In the same way, my spirit can respond non-verbally to the Word of God. As I embrace it, delight in it, my body may respond by shaking with joy, which is an expression of my spirit dancing with joy. I may laugh,—why had I not seen that before?—the eyes of my spirit have seen something more of my glorious Lord His love for me, my inheritance—glory to God!

I will pray in tongues. As I do so, focusing on a particular scripture, it will be as if the muscles of that scripture are growing stronger. I can ask God to reveal more about it. While praying in tongues, thoughts will arise about it such as,—'Yes, this is for you—delight to put it to work—at home'. I will receive a deeper understanding of its **awesome character**, for example, how it cannot fail to work—hallelujah. The Holy Spirit can take hold of that precious Word and reveal it to me as I need it right now—glory to God!

I will dwell in the Word richly, delight in it, when by myself and with others. Like Paul, 'I will sing with the spirit, and I will also sing with the understanding (1Cor 14:15)—glory to God, I am being built up.

Live it—language

What joy it will be to talk about the Word, to share the new revelations received and for others to catch its life. My delight in it, my enthusiasm will be so evident. It will be infectious.

Others will sense this dynamic in their spirit and be drawn to know it for themselves and be drawn to You—glory to God. Also, my prayers will be more than just words. They will be rooted from deep within and be effective. They will work—hallelujah!

Live it—lifestyle

I am full of the living Word. Whatever the situation, whatever the problem, I know that the truth living in me, will release the solution, the wisdom, the love, the healing, the miracle—hallelujah. There is no limit to our God.

Now

Today, I will trust You with all my heart and trust the power of Your life within. Wherever I go, I will be ready to bring life, to be the answer to any problem. I am loaded with the living Word, I am loaded with life. I know there will be many divine encounters. Many will be blessed by Your life flowing from me.

Triumphantly

What joy is in my spirit. You know the people I will be meeting today. You have planned it all. You know that their lives are going to be transformed through our encounter. You are going to be so glorified today. It will be an exciting day today.

Part II

In HIM –
so much MORE!

This is a revelation the Holy Spirit has given me about our Lord Jesus Christ, about the Living Word. It has enabled me to understand so much more than I dreamed of, to increasingly live a life like His. It is not a new truth, the scriptures have always been there, simply a revelation of them. It is my prayer that as you read these pages, and devour the truths, you will not just see your true identity in Jesus and embrace it, but live in it, so fulfilling the glorious destiny He has prepared for you before the foundation of the world.

In HIM –so much MORE!

Contents

Chapter 1. So Much MORE 60

Chapter 2. In Him—Before I Was Born on earth 70
        a) God's blue print for man..70
        b) We were in Christ..77
        c) Dominion restored...80
        d) Hidden in Him 82

Chapter 3. In Him—In His Soul—In the Word 84
        a) What/Who is this Living Word? 85
        b) Fertile ground for this awesome living word!..........88
        c) Receive your miracle,—step into the glory of.
           the Word 93
        d) Other ways our spirits can touch and embrace.
           the glory of the Word..96

Chapter 4. In Him—In His Spirit...100
        a) Aware of the dynamic of His spirit in the
           created world 100
        b) In His Spirit manifest in His breath, wind 102
        c) In His Spirit manifest as fire in us 104

Chapter 5. In Him—In His Body 110

Chapter 6. In Him—Living in His rest 113

Chapter 7. Respond -- Just as Jesus Did 119

1

so much MORE...!

"....I have come that they may have life, and that they may have it more abundantly." John 10:10. Does this describe most believers? No. Many do not live in the joy and victory He has provided for us, because they do not know how the truths of the bible can become alive within them. Also, of those who do know them, many seek abundance in material or spiritual terms. When blessed, prosperous or healed, they say, 'yes this is the abundant life'. But these are only the trimmings!!! This true abundant life is what Jesus lived, and it made Him have joy more than all His companions, 'exultant joy and gladness above and beyond Your companions', Heb 1:9 AMP. It is a joy found only through knowing His love for us, and embracing <u>with joy</u> the unique glorious path He has already prepared for us, Eph 2:10. We discover that we are <u>blessed to be a blessing</u>, Gen 12:2. He is a life-giving spirit, 1Cor 15:45. When we are born again we are born of a life-giving spirit. We become <u>life-giving spirits. His life flowing through us bringing life wherever we go</u>, Ez 47:9. This is the joy of Zion for each of us—the real abundant life.

Basic truths to know within

If we are born again, God has equipped us to live such a life. We need to know within that the same Divine life that was in Jesus is in us. He gave it to us so that we could continue His work, do the same things He did and even greater, John 14:12. In Part I, 'My True Identity', this ground is dealt with thoroughly, so that key basic truths become alive within. I recommend that you feast and digest the truths it covers. We need to know within for example, that we are <u>loved perfectly</u>, 1John 4:18, so <u>God is our security, not man</u>. That <u>our old life is dead</u>, Rom 6:3-6, the old selfish heart of stone has been removed, and has been <u>replaced by</u> <u>a new heart of love</u>, Ez 36:26: We must know that we are <u>new creations</u> born of the Word of God, that all of Jesus is within us! We must know our authority, so the enemy is no longer a problem. Thus we abide in Him, totally trusting the Living Word. When filled with the spirit, not only are all the gifts there for us, but a Divine fire is burning within enabling us to release rivers of living water wherever we are, John 7:38. <u>Our joy is for Him to be glorified</u>!

I have discovered that once a person has truly yielded their life—110% to our Lord, the most crucial basic doctrine for them to take hold of, and indeed <u>celebrate</u>, is <u>the death of their old life</u> with Jesus on the cross, 'knowing this, that our old man was crucified with Him', Rom 6:6. Only then can they start truly living His new life which has been given to them; the Divine resurrection life, with a new heart burning with love. Few Christians have embraced it with joy! Consequently their lives are a continual struggle with their old problems, weaknesses, addictions, fear, unbelief, sicknesses, pride etc. They hope one day they might be free. Not realising that **<u>it is already done</u>**, Gal 5:1. We are destroyed not through the enemy, but through lack of knowledge, Hos 4:6. But if the glory of this truth is taught and imparted from the start, the Christian life becomes exciting straight away. <u>New believers</u> can expect to live in the miraculous, and they are not disappointed. Again and again I have seen this happen in Africa in Zambia and Tanzania, in India and Pakistan. Even illiterate people, born again one day, with these revelations living in them, the next day are not just leading people to Christ, but healing the sick! They testify of the lame walking, healing people of TB, diabetes, blindness etc: I have such testimonies on DVD.

Your goal?

What is your goal? God makes it very clear what He wants of us. We are all called to live as He did. Jesus said, '<u>Just as</u> You {Father} sent Me into the world, I also have sent them into the world,' John 17:18 AMP. John wrote, 'He who says he abides in Him ought himself also to <u>walk just as He walked</u>', 1John 2:6. People were amazed and astonished at Jesus, so they should be of you and me! What has gone wrong? When God made man in the Garden of Eden, He made him perfectly, in His image and in His likeness, to function just as He did. I am convinced 100% of man's brain was active before the fall. His Spirit was open to

God. I gather now only about 10% of it is functioning, 90% is relatively dormant. At the fall man was separated from God. His spirit died. We could say, despite all the achievements of man, spiritually we have de-evolved, become increasingly less aware of the spiritual life, dynamic, which is unfortunate as the real us is a spirit being. I believe that the Holy Spirit can teach us how to access and indeed live in this realm of the spirit, just as Jesus did!

What is your goal? When I was at Bible College I became aware that most students hoped to live a good Christian life and to have a ministry. But this is far below what God has in His heart for us, which is to be <u>just as He was</u> on earth. Jesus is the Word of God Who became flesh, John 1:14. His life was an expression of the Living Word, a continual release of Divine life, miracles flowed from Him. I decided, I was not going to be satisfied until my life was <u>as His</u>. Not <u>like</u> Him, me trying to emulate Him, but <u>as</u> Him, releasing the same life from within as He did. Praise God, there are an increasing number of ministries that do expect and are blessed with miracles. There is great joy when some occur. It is indeed wonderful. But with Jesus again and again, <u>all who came to Him were healed</u>, Matt 15:30-31. I decided that this is what I would go for. Jesus said, **"If you can believe, all things are possible to him who believes."** Mark 9:23. I have seen this happen on a number of occasions. But there is so much more. I long to see this happen always, including the dead being raised (Matt 10:8). We set our goals. The more we expect of God in line with the Scriptures, the more He delights to do in our lives! Not all of us are able to go into all the world, Mark 16:15, but wherever He has placed us He expects rivers of living water to flow from our lives; His mighty miraculous hand to be so evident as we shine as lights, Matt 5:16. What is your goal?

Understanding our infinite 'immeasurable' Almighty GOD

We have developed a sophisticated way of analysing the bible. Unfortunately Almighty God does not fit into our neat intellectual boxes. Such a study of God has been rather like someone out to study the sun. They spend years making an excellent camera, able to pick up extraordinary details, and examine them, the variations of the colour, how it changes etc: and then say they know what the sun is like. No, no, no, their analysis may tell them what it looks like from earth, but ignores key aspects. It tells them little of its heat, its power, the ways it affects gravity, enables life etc:

God is so much more glorious than the sun which he created. To come to know Almighty God, would it not be better to focus on Him, simply with the tools He has provided, the Word of God which is spirit and it is life, John 6:63, and the Holy Spirit, who guides us into all truth, John 16:13? Thereby we can have revelation knowledge; revelation given by the Holy Spirit which can flourish, revelation on revelation! By so doing, a spiritual logic with its own Biblical criteria emerges through which we can assess the validity of a revelation. It involves three factors, **firstly**, the extent to which it reveals the depths of a scripture and is consistent with or indeed opens up others. **Secondly** a witness within confirming the reality of the scripture or that the understanding is right despite perhaps, it making no carnal logical sense! Rom 8:16 Alternatively an unease may arise from within as we know it is inconsistent with other scriptures. (This must be distinguished from a religious stronghold, which can cause a deep rejection of the revelation on the basis of a long held unbiblical understanding or tradition which is deemed more valid that the Word of God, more valid than God!!! Some churches even today do not embrace the Holy Spirit, tongues, or miracles. Thus they prevent their members from stepping into the unsearchable riches of that arena). Paul speaks much of the spiritual realm inaccessible by the mere senses but only through the Spirit. 'But as it is written; "Eye has not seen, not ear heard, nor have entered into the heart of man the things which God has prepared for those who love Him." But God has revealed them to us through His Spirit. For the Spirit searches all things, yes, the deep things of God . . . . Now we have received, not the spirit of the world, but <u>the Spirit who is from God, that we might know the things that have been freely given to us by God</u>. These things we also speak, not in words which man's wisdom teaches but which the Holy Spirit teaches, comparing spiritual things with spiritual.' 1Cor 2:9-14. Thus Paul said, 'my speech and my preaching were not with persuasive words of human wisdom, but in demonstration of the Spirit and of power, that **your faith should not be in the wisdom of men but in the power of God**, 1Cor 2:4-5.

Thirdly, and possibly the most crucial criterion, is the extent to which it enables the revelation to <u>become alive within</u>, Heb 4:12, <u>so our lives express it</u>. What is important is not how much we know intellectually, (which can easily lead to pride, 'knowledge puffs up, but love edifies,' 1Cor 8:1), but how much we live? Do we love like Jesus did? Do we walk by faith or by sight? Are miracles a regular occurrence in our lives as they were in His? To the religious mind such a criterion is irrelevant, but not to God who wants each of our lives to be as Jesus. Since I have been feasting on these truths, my absolute confidence in the Living Word, my faith and boldness have increased phenomenally. I have just returned from Pakistan where God opened doors. One night I preached to twelve thousand people, half of whom were Muslim. Well over three thousand were saved, hundreds healed. On the last night there I was ministering to a thousand precious souls. Over six hundred were saved plus exciting miracles. An elderly man testified how one side of his body had been paralysed, and he had been unable to speak. He was waving his arm as he walked on the platform unaided, singing a Christian song. (This all happened in less than fifteen minutes—my plane home was due to leave in four hours!) **For the Kingdom of God is not in word but in power! 1Cor 4:20 we have had enough talk. The 'world' longs to see it lived, Rom 8:19. Let us not be satisfied with anything less than His love, glory and power being manifest daily through our lives.**

Key to it all

Essential to such a walk is a <u>**radical approach to the Word,**</u> namely seeing it <u>**as the Word of Almighty God**</u>!—not open to argument. If Jesus came into your room, in all His Presence, glory, with perfect love glowing from His eyes, and said, 'You are healed' Is 53:5, you would rise to your feet celebrating your healing. If He said, 'Before I formed you in the womb I knew you; before you were born I sanctified you;' Jer 1:5, You would respond, 'Hallelujah, thank you Lord, that I was so special to you even before I was born.' Your confidence in His love for you would be at a new depth, and so your security in Him. You would not dream of saying His words were theoretical, or that it is just a picture, or just a thought, which can then be put to one side and ignored.' ('Religion' has regarded such an exercise as legitimate. Doing so is dangerous ground, as it gives license to the enemy to question the validity of any scripture that is not picked up by the current 'sophisticated camera' or religious box! He used the same tactic back in the Garden of Eden, 'God did not really mean what He said, . . . ' Gen 3:1,4. Such a person may want to argue that, 'Christ in you' is just a thought, or merely theoretical. What about Jesus being raised from the dead!') No, no, no, let the Word of God be the Word of God, not open to debate, not open to man to tamper with. Recognise that every truth, in the spirit is a fact, <u>**it is done**</u>, it is a spiritual reality. Indeed, so much of our inheritance does not refer to the future, it is described in the present or past tense. Eg: we <u>are new creations</u>

2Cor 5:17, we <u>have been crucified</u> with Christ, Rom 6:6 — glory! We <u>have been made kings</u> and priests! Rev 1:6. <u>It is our responsibility to see that that truth becomes our life</u>.

How to walk by faith and not by sight

Most Christians do have faith, but it rarely seems to work for them. They try to strengthen their faith, but with minimal results. The issue is not their faith, but their unbelief which negates their faith. They look at the circumstances, and conclude it is not so, and rationalise their unbelief, eg: 'miracles finished with the apostles'. They are walking not by faith but by sight, 2Cor 5:7. They have given place to the demonic spirit of unbelief as did Adam and eve in the Garden of Eden. (Unbelief is not just not believing, but believing in something contrary to the Word of God. God calls unbelief a sin, John 16:9. It was because of their 'evil heart of unbelief, that a generation of Israelites did not enter the promised land, Heb 3:12,19.) A picture has helped me to clarify this. If a particular promise is like a cart, it only needs an ox (our faith) to pull it — and it will move easily. But if at the opposite end of the cart there is another ox called unbelief pulling in the opposite direction it will not move. No matter how big the ox (faith) is, if a similar sized ox of unbelief is pulling in the opposite direction it still will not move. A double minded man can expect nothing from God, James 1:6-7. All that is required is to unhitch the 'unbelief' ox. They may try to fill their minds with the Word of God, but it is hard, as circumstances, the pain, the fear speaks loudly, strengthening their unbelief. **How much better and easier, to see and understand that the living Word of God is of a different, superior order to anything in the natural. Thereby, any alien mindset or even circumstance becomes irrelevant.**

In Him

'In Him', is the focus of this book. I have heard learned Christians refer to 'in Him' as 'positional' or 'theoretical', thus avoiding exploring its extraordinary implications and how we can live in their light. What does it mean? Can we live 'in Him'? Surely we can, as Paul uses this expression so much, eg: 'you are complete in Him.' Col 2:10. Through feasting on the relevant scriptures the Holy Spirit has revealed much to me. In so doing, other frequently passed over scriptures have begun to make sense, spiritual sense, and so can be lived! One of these is, 'as **He is** so are we in this world'. Note, it does not say as He was, but as <u>He is</u> — now. This scripture alone, immediately takes us out of those carnal boxes, not just of time—<u>He is</u>,—but into the measureless capacities of God which He demonstrated in creation and when on earth—glory!

I see 'in Him' as a consummation of God's heart for man. In Genesis we are told that <u>God made man in His own image, to multiply</u>. 'Then God blessed them, and God said to them, "Be fruitful and multiply; fill the earth and subdue it; have dominion over the fish of the sea . . .' Gen1:28. In the gospels Jesus gave us a beautiful picture of our new creation life, He being the vine and we the branches, the fruit bearing part of the vine, indeed, expected to bear much fruit, John 15:5. Our life is no longer separate as it was in the Old Testament, but we are joined, 1Cor 6:17, and can 'abide' day and night, enjoying a 'vital union', John 15:5. AMP. The Message describes our relationship as 'intimate and organic'. God wants us to have a knowledge of Him far beyond our dreams! Jesus' life bore extraordinary fruit. So did Paul's. **So can the life of each one of us!**

The challenge

The revelation that Christ is in us is glorious, Col 1:27, the perfection of Almighty God within (Col 2:9), our bodies being His temple, 1Cor 6:19. It is almost incomprehensible even to our spirits, yet it is easier to take hold of than us being 'in Him'. If He is in **<u>me</u>**, **'<u>I</u>'** may still be the focus—'**<u>I</u>**' am the one carrying Him. But, being '**<u>in Him</u>**' is far deeper and richer. It implies being <u>totally yielded to **Him**, fused with **Him**, one with **Him**</u>. (This is true humility.) Yet, this only seems daunting to the natural mind. When we understand the supernatural dynamics or what/Who the Word of God is, it becomes so exciting—that the Living Word has inherent within it all that Jesus is, that it is outside time, perfect etc: Not constrained by traditional boxes, we can delight in letting it reveal its secrets.

You may say why walk on water when there is dry ground? Our God is a God who walks on water. To know Him we need to delight in all aspects of Him. If you are content with your present understanding, this book is not for you. But, if on the other hand, in your heart you have a deep conviction that what you know now, although it may be glorious, is minimal compared to what He has for you; after all, **we are <u>all called to be as Jesus</u>, let us ardently pursue the 'so much more'. Just imagine if every Christian was walking as Jesus. What an impact he had in the world. If that was multiplied by all of us, the world would be a very different place.** <u>He has placed each one of us in a specific family,</u>

in a specific country at a specific time because He has planned that each one of us will transform it, bringing His light, His Kingdom into that area, and beyond, **as Jesus did!**

Areas explored . . . .

Chapter 2 delves into **what it means to be a spirit being**. A number of scriptures reveal to us that our spirits existed before we were born, indeed before time began. 'For those whom He foreknew [of whom He was aware and loved beforehand], He also destined from the beginning to be molded into the image of His Son [and share inwardly His likeness], that He might become the firstborn among many brethren, Rom 8:29 AMP. This suggests that we were in God, with God when He created the world and so much more . . . !

Jesus when on earth was 100% God and 100% man. Jesus as the Son of Man, like us had a spirit, soul and body, 1Thes 5:23. The next three chapters explore the significance of being 'in Him' in these three areas, in His Spirit, His soul and His body. His soul is the essence of who He is, the Living Word. So I have started with 'in Him', in Jesus the Living Word. This is **Chapter 3.** 'And the Word became flesh and dwelt among us, and we beheld His glory, the glory as of the only begotten of the Father, full of grace and truth', John 1:14. Scriptures elucidating the nature of this glorious awesome Living Word are explored. We see that to truly embrace these dynamics, requires more than a yielded heart; one that says, 'Yes Lord', with joy. Having seen the extraordinary nature of the Word of God, you will now be able to receive your miracle, by simply stepping into the glory of a particular truth. (Other ways to access the depths of a truth, and to enable your spiritual muscles to grow strong, follow.)

'Heal the sick, cleanse the lepers, raise the dead, cast out demons. Freely you have received, freely give.' Matt 10:8. We can now go on to focus on facets of the Holy Spirit, which will enable you to set others free, as Jesus did, Luke 4:18, and you will find doing so to be your joy—a marvellous joy of Zion!

Chapter 4 looks at being in Him, as Spirit. I have not dwelt on the nature of the Holy Spirit or the gifts, which is ground well documented, but rather, on less well trodden areas . . . . ! For example our understanding of the extent to which His spirit is active in the world, in nature, in things, has been given little attention. Despite the fact we know that dead, dry bones had to respond as Ezekiel commanded them to "<u>hear</u> the word of the LORD", Ez 37:4 (in the Hebrew the word 'hear ' means 'listen attentively'); Rocks had to respond, Ex17:6. Storms had to obey the Word of Jesus, Mark 4:39. Diseased bodies had to come into alignment! Matt 15:30-31. Also, we are told that He upholds all things (present tense) through the power of His Word, Heb 1:3. How does God want us to live in the light of these truths?

He revealed His Presence and power not just through His words, but in His breath, which is the next part of this section. When operating in the spirit, <u>our breath has the same power</u>!

God is a consuming fire. This is the third aspect of the spirit we delight in. If we are filled with the Spirit, <u>that same fire, or Divine energy, is burning in us</u>, Matt 3:11. What does the Bible tell us about this Divine fire? It is not just manifest in <u>passionate love</u>, but also in <u>a righteous anger</u> at the works of the enemy. Being in Him, in this holy fire, suggests becoming one with it, fused with it; so <u>we are flames of fire</u>, Heb 1:7…! Surely this is the essence of a revival church.

Chapter 5 deals with 'in Him' as in His physical body, 'members of His body, of His flesh and of His bones', Eph 5:30. <u>We delight in strange assertions</u>, like when Jesus was on earth He declared He dwelt in heaven, John 3:13. What did He mean? If we can understand what He meant, it should be the same for us, as we too are seated in heavenly places! Eph 2:6.

If the truths of the previous chapters have been absorbed, digested, we discover we have entered His rest, a glorious union with Him, conscious of living in His Holy Presence, Heb 4:10. This is **Chapter 6**. What He is, we are. So we can make similar declarations to those He made!

Chapter 7 takes it further. If we 'know' we are as He is, we will <u>delight</u> in being continually prompted by the Father as He was, Ps 40:8. Consequently we will respond to situations and act in a very similar manner to the way He did. Indeed we are assured that, "he who believes in Me, the works that I do he will do also; and greater works than these he will do, . . ."! John 14:12.

These truths can become a reality

This is not a book to be read straight through. The heart of each chapter is in the scriptures, the truths they contain. 'Your words were found, and I ate them, and Your word was to me the joy and rejoicing of my heart', Jer 15:16. Imagine a table specially prepared for you, Ps 23:5. Each chapter is like a meal, full of exquisite food (truths). Take time over each 'meal', each chapter, before proceeding to the next, so that the glory of the revelations will be digested, be imparted deep into your spirit. When you go through them a second time, the previous revelations will be as a floor for even richer ones!

I have sought to present these truths, to serve them on attractive 'plates', so that you can easily meditate on them, wonder at and in them, Josh 1:8. With some scriptures there are brackets like this, { . . . }, which I have added to clarify the text. **With joy declare what has been written in bold under each**, which will enable the very life of the truths to become personal. Through speaking them, your spirit will hear, and thus your faith grow stronger and stronger, Rom 10:17. Underneath in italics in brackets, there is an elaboration the Holy Spirit has whispered in my ear. As you listen to Him, He will reveal to you more and more of their mysteries; deeper and deeper revelations! As they become alive and vibrant within, you will find not only the way you speak has changed, but **you will be doing just as Jesus did**—glory!

2

IN HIM —
BEFORE I WAS BORN ON EARTH

a) God's blue print for man is for him to be and function as He did Gen 1:26-27.

In the Old Testament, in Ps 82, God refers to His judges, as 'gods' ('elohim' in Hebrew), 'I said, "You are gods, and all of you are children of the Most High,"' Ps 82:6. Jesus confirmed the validity of this psalm in John 10:34. Judges were His special people at the time. He was angry with them because they abused their position, and were not living as 'gods', as His special people. He said, that if they continued like this, they would die like mere men, Ps 82:7. I believe God is saying the same but with more ardour to us today, to His special people who unlike them are born again. "I have now given you the very same life that was in Jesus, to be sons like Him, He was the 'firstborn among many brethren', Rom 8:29. He is not physically on earth. He has passed the baton on to you, so live as He did!" We have a choice, to rise up to this awesome calling, or to suffer and die as ordinary fallen human beings!

Being a son of God!

He (Christ) is the image of the invisible God, Col 1:15. For it pleased [the Father] that all the divine fullness (the sum total of the divine perfection, powers and attributes) should dwell in Him permanently, Col 1:19. AMP

Religion has watered down the significance of being a son of God. If a lawyer came into your room and told you there had been some mistake, and you were in fact a son or daughter of the king or queen, you would know immediately what a change this would involve. Poverty would no longer be an issue. You would have a new life with people who held power. In fact the bible tells us we have been made kings, Rev 1:6. 'Where the word of a king is, there is power,' Ecc 8:4. Our words have power.

Much, much more than that: If Jesus entered your house and said to you: 'Now you are a child of God.' 1John 3:2, 'You are His offspring,' Acts 17:28, having been born again of the **perfect incorruptible seed of the word of God**,' 1Pet 1:23; you now have the same DNA that God has. The significance is far greater than that of being in an earthly royal family. It even affects our physical bodies. It is almost too glorious for our minds to comprehend, that the infinite, supernatural, Almighty God has made His home in our bodies, John 14:23. They are His temples, 1Cor 6:19. We are no longer ordinary human beings, sustained by blood, Lev 17:11, but by the Divine, supernatural resurrection life, Rom 6:4-5. The Holy Spirit now quickens our mortal bodies, Rom 8:11. How powerful is this divine life working within us? It is the same mighty power that worked in Jesus, that raised Him from the dead! Eph 1:19-20. As our spirits embrace and absorb these truths, our bodies no longer respond as 'normal' human beings. We learn how we can live in divine health, 1Pet 2:24. If we drink anything poisonous it does not harm us. Paul was bitten by a viper but it did not affect him, Acts 28:3-6. I have heard testimonies of Muslims who have become Christians, forced to drink poison, but it did not affect them. I have been in many countries and eaten many strange things, (some of which I have been told what they are, caterpillars, flying ants, intestines, mice ... !)

We are told as believers, sons of God, as we lay hands on the sick they Will recover, Mark 16:17-18. As we do, something of the spirit is released from our body, destroying the sickness and bringing life to what is dead. We are exhorted to operate the God kind of faith, Mark 11:22; like God, to call things that do not exist as though they did, Rom 4:17; like Jesus to speak to storms. Even nature, the creation longs for us to live as sons of God. 'The earnest expectation of the creation, eagerly waits for the revealing of the sons (huios) of God, Rom 8:19.

Jesus the perfect model, the Son of God

Jesus on earth was The Son (huios) of God. ('Huios' refers to the maturity of the relationship, in His likeness—in Him! Paul uses it of us in Rom 8:14, ' as many as are led by the Spirit of God, these are sons (huios) of God.') As such, He was continually aware of being **in** the Father and the Father **in** Him, John 10:38. 'He who has seen Me has seen the Father' John 14:9. I and My Father are **one**, John 10:30. He delighted to do His Father's will, Ps 40:8. <u>His life on earth was a demonstration of what it means to be absolutely yielded to God.</u> Consequently, He was able to embrace the destiny God had ordained for Him. It was the same for Paul. When starting a letter he often referred to himself as a <u>bondservant</u> or slave of Jesus Christ, called to be an apostle, (eg: Rom 1:1). This is true maturity. The more we get to know and trust our Lord as the Living Word, the more we see that His purpose for us is infinitely greater than any we could dream for our self. So <u>with joy</u> we say, '<u>Yes Lord</u>'. Oh, 'the glory of being a love slave!'

His passion for us to be as He is; sons of God

This was our Lord's prayer. "I.. pray . . . that they all may be one, as You Father, are in Me, and I in You; that they also may be one in us, that the world may believe that You sent Me." John 17:20.21.

He longs for us not just to know how His heart beats, but to be truly **in Him**, so that <u>our heart is fused with His</u>. As we delight ourselves in Him He gives us the desires of our heart, Ps37:4. <u>We taste the joys of Zion</u>. We discover we have Divine impulses; His love burning within to set others free. Further—more, 'They are abundantly satisfied with the fullness of Your house, and You give them drink from <u>the river of Your pleasures</u>, Ps 36:8. What a privilege, to represent Him on earth; to know we are called and equipped so that we can function just as Jesus did. This is the essence of His calling on our lives, and our responsibility, wherever He has placed us, to accomplish it!

Is this possible?   Yes, because <u>God made us to be essentially spirit beings as He is</u>. So we can begin to understand 'the unending (boundless, unfathomable, incalculable, and exhaustless) riches of Christ [wealth which no human being could have searched out], Eph 3:8 AMP. We can come to know His love for us, 'that you may be filled [through all your being] unto all the fullness of God [may have the richest measure of the divine Presence, and become a body wholly filled and flooded with God Himself]! Eph 3:19 AMP. Now to Him who is able to do exceedingly abundantly above all that we ask or think, <u>according to the power that works in us</u>, to Him be glory . . . Eph 3:20-21. What follows is an attempt to lay aside religious boxes, so that the very life and glory of the Word of God can be embraced and lived. Let it be a feast for your spirit so that your life will be a sign and wonder, Is 8:18 —Hallelujah!

God is a Spirit being and essentially so are we

God, who is Spirit, John 4:24, breathed into us the very breath or spirit of life, Gen 2:7, so that man could know Him. Adam's body and soul (mind, will and emotions) had no life in them until spirit was imparted from God. Our spirit or heart is the essence of who we are, of our personality. Num 14:24 speaks of Caleb who had 'a different spirit in him', from that of the unbelieving Israelites. It was this which caused him to 'follow Me fully'. Only he and Joshua entered the promised land!

The spirit of a man is eternal, as God is. Christians know this applies to our future, that when we die we will go to either heaven or hell. But they are not so familiar with the scriptures (see below) that reveal to us that we were with God, before time began. Eg: 'He chose us in Him before the foundation of the world, Eph 1:4. Can your spirit grasp this? That we were truly in Him, yet in no way did that affect Who He is, His Presence, purity, absolute perfection, glory? As we lay aside earth bound logic, our spirit can sore with Him.

Our spirits can comprehend mysteries!

It is hard enough to take in that Almighty God loves me perfectly, that I am so treasured by Him, 1 John 4:18. It is too marvellous for the finite natural mind to comprehend that He loves billions of people with that same perfect love, knowing even the numbers of hairs in their head, but He does, Matt 10:30. **This is our God!** It is even harder, yet even more glorious that He knew and loved the real me, my spirit being, when I was in Him before I was born. As this dawns in my heart, I discover a **new dimension of security in Him.** He loved me before I was born; loves me while on earth and will do so for all eternity. Rooted and grounded in His love Eph 3:17, takes on a new meaning, that my true lineage goes back to before time began! — hallelujah!

Secondly, if we were in Him before time began, we were surely with Him as He created the world; indeed, throughout the Old Testament, experiencing in some way what He went through. Similarly we were in Christ when He was on earth, crucified, in hell and raised. Thus, when the Bible speaks of us (who are born again), as being 'hidden in Him' Col 3:3, it is not so strange, so unfamiliar. Indeed to be exhorted to function as Jesus did on earth does not seem so impossible. This does not fit intellectual boxes, but neither do many scriptures about Jesus.

For example, we are told that we can now understand 'the riches of the glory of this mystery', which is <u>Christ in you,</u> Col 1:27. Glory, He is now in us, and if He is in us, so is the Father who is in Him, John 14:10, yet both are in heaven! **We can either let such truths confuse us as it will the carnal unrenewed mind Rom 12:2, or excite us!!!!!**

Declarations
<u>We are spirit beings as He is</u>

Gen 2:7	And the LORD God formed man of the dust of the ground, and breathed into his nostrils the breath or spirit of life; and man became a living being. AMP
Ecc 12:7	{When we die} ... Then shall the dust [out of which God made man's body] return to the earth as it was, <u>and the spirit shall **return** to God Who gave it</u>. AMP

I am essentially a spirit being
(Unlike other creation, I breathed My spirit into man so that he could relate to Me.)

Jer 1:5	<u>Before</u> I formed you in the womb <u>I knew you; before you were born I sanctified you</u>;
Rom 8:29	For those whom He foreknew [of whom <u>He was aware and loved beforehand</u>], He also destined <u>from the beginning</u> [foreordaining them] to be molded into the image of His Son [and share inwardly His likeness], that He might become the firstborn among many brethren, AMP.

My spirit, my real self, is eternal—existed (and was known by You) before I was born
(as well as when you die.)

Eph 1:4	... He chose us in Him <u>before the foundation of the world</u>,
2Tim 1:9	who has saved us and called us with a holy calling, not according to our works, but according to His own purpose and grace which was <u>given to us in Christ Jesus before time began</u>,

I was with God before the world began.
(Your true lineage—the real you, your spirit was hidden in Me.)—glory!

In Him — so much MORE! 75

Prov 8:30 {This speaks of wisdom or Jesus, John 1:1-2}
.... I was daily His delight, rejoicing always before Him,
John 17:24 ... "You loved Me before the foundation of the world."
I know Jesus had a relationship of love and of joy with His Father
(Before you were born I loved you and you loved me, Rom 8:29. In the same way I have loved, known and sanctified billions of people before they were ever born. 'Impossible!' — I AM GOD. Each is My workmanship, My work of art. Now you are as Me on earth, so love, honour and delight in the uniqueness of all whom you encounter. Do all you can so that the unique flavour of My glory in each one, will be manifest to all.)

In Him our Creator God

Gen 1:2-3 ... And the Spirit of God was hovering over the face of the waters.
Then God said, "Let there be light", and there was light.
I know God creates (in the Presence of the Holy Spirit), with words.
(I see what I want to create within and speak it. In those words all My power --- the power of Almighty God — is activated, channelled, and it comes into being in all its perfection.)

Gen 1:31 Then God saw everything that He had made, and indeed it was very good.
**I was with Him as he created the beautiful world
I know the joy of making beautiful things**
(Your real nature is as Me, to be creative, to delight in creating beautiful things, not mediocre things, or that which causes pain and suffering.)

In Him as a Person with emotions

Gen 6:6 And the LORD was sorry that He had made man on the earth, and He was <u>grieved in His heart</u>.
Ex 32:10 "Now therefore, let Me alone, that My wrath may burn hot against them..
I know the anguish He felt when man, His special treasure, went his own way

(Because they turned away from Me, I could not reveal My heart and bless them as abundantly as I longed to.)

Song 8:6   For love is as strong as death . . . its flames are flames of fire, a most vehement flame.

Zech 8:2   I am zealous for Zion with great zeal; with great fervor I am zealous for her.

I know He is passionate—there is a fire burning in His Spirit

(It is unquenchable. My glorious Divine purposes will be fulfilled and I long for you to be part of them.)

Is 55:7   Let the wicked forsake his way, . . . let him return to the LORD, and He will have mercy on him; . . . for He will abundantly pardon.

Zeph 3:17   ". . . . He will rejoice over you with gladness, He will quiet you with His love, He will rejoice over you with singing."

I know the joy when he {man} responds

(It thrills My heart. Oh the joy! I want you to know such intimacy, even ecstasy in our relationship. And when you enable someone else to taste it too, you experience one of the most beautiful joys of Zion, 1Pet 1:8, Luke 10:17, 21.)

Jer 3:14,   "<u>Return, O backsliding children</u>," says the LORD; "<u>for I am married to you</u>. I will take you, one from a city and two from a family, and I will bring you to Zion.

Luke 4:18   "The Spirit of the LORD is upon Me, because He has anointed Me to preach the gospel to the poor; He has sent Me to heal the broken-hearted, to proclaim liberty to the captives and recovery of sight to the blind, to set at liberty those who are oppressed;"

I know how His heart yearns for us to know the blessed life He has prepared for us

(I have such a zeal for all to return to Me, to be set free from the oppression they are living under, and thus enabling the glory of the Kingdom of God to be established on earth.)

b) **We were in Christ when He was on earth**

Can we be both in the Father and in Jesus at the same time? Yes. This is no problem in the spirit. Although at the time, the Father was in heaven and Jesus was on the earth, they were one. Jesus said, "I and My Father are one" John 10:30. He spoke of Himself, "the Son of Man who is in heaven", John 3:13 (See more when 'in Him in His body' is explored!)

Matt 17:5 "This is My beloved Son, in whom I am well pleased. <u>Hear Him!</u>"
I know that all the power of God—undisputable dominion was in the words he spoke—things had to obey
(When I said 'Hear Him', I was not just speaking to My disciples, but to all creation; human bodies, fish, trees, rocks, storms, all, would hear Him and have to obey.)

Matt 15:30 Then great multitudes came to Him, having with them the lame, blind, mute, maimed, and many others; and they laid them down as Jesus' feet, and He healed them.

John 11:43 {Lazarus had been dead for four days} He cried with a loud voice, "<u>Lazarus, come forth!</u>"
I was in him as He demonstrated his love, healing the sick, raising the dead
(You know the perfection and power of the resurrection life released in My Words and through My touch. This was a natural expression of who I AM. There was no possibility it could not work.)

Mark 4:39 Then He arose and <u>rebuked the wind,</u> and <u>said to the sea,</u> "Peace be still!" And the wind ceased and there was a great calm.
　　　　—when He stilled the storm
(The disciples were amazed, but you are not, as I, the Son of God, had spoken.)

Matt 9:36 But when He saw the multitudes, He was moved with compassion for them,

Matt 14:18 He said, "Bring them {five loaves and two fishes} here to Me."

        —when He multiplied the loaves and fishes
        (My compassion was burning deep within.)

I understood what he meant when He said,

John 8:12   I am the light of the world.
                  (My light defines the situation. The natural world is in darkness, ignorance.)

John 6:48   I am the bread of life.
                  (I, the living Word, am the true food of the spirit.)

John 11:25   I am the resurrection and the life.
                  (My life on earth demonstrated this Divine supernatural life.)

I died, went to hell, defeated Satan, and rose with Him

Rom 6:3-6 makes it very clear that our old self was crucified, buried and raised with Him. The Scriptures do not say that God separated my spirit from Him when He defeated Satan and then returned it to be in Him when He was raised. No, we were surely in Him throughout, including when He defeated the enemy!)

Ez 36:26   ... I will <u>take the heart of stone out of your flesh</u> and give you a heart of flesh.

Rom 6:6   knowing this, that <u>our old man was crucified with Him</u>, that the body of sin might be done away with, that we should no longer be slaves of sin.

Gal 2:20   <u>I have been crucified with Christ</u>; it is no longer I who live, but Christ lives in me;
                I was with Him, when He was crucified
                (The old self-centred independent person you used to be, energized by a selfish 'heart of stone' was crucified. That person full of fear, pride and unbelief is no more. Celebrate this glorious fact. With joy mortify [Rom 8:13] any trace of the old life that might emerge. Praising Me declare the truth that it is dead. Given no oxygen it will soon disintegrate.)

Gal 6:14	But God forbid that I should boast except in the cross of our Lord Jesus Christ, by whom the world has been crucified to me, and I to the world. **Hallelujah—thank You for setting me free from the world** (What bound you has no more power over you. The world's attractions of status, lust etc, have become hollow, 'rubbish' to you. They have been replaced by the joys of Zion!)
Col 2:15	Having disarmed principalities and powers, He made a public spectacle of them, triumphing over them in it.
Heb 2:14	. . . through death He might destroy him who had the power of death, that is, the devil. **I was in You as You defeated the enemy** (You went to hell with Me; with Me defeated not ordinary demons, but their master Satan himself)
Rom 6:4-5	we were <u>buried with Him</u> . . . , that <u>just as Christ was raised from the dead</u> by the glory of the Father, even so <u>we also should walk in newness of life</u>. For if we have been united together in the likeness of His death, <u>certainly</u> we also shall be in the likeness of His resurrection. **I was raised with Him** (I was made sin, but <u>rose with no trace of sin in Me</u>, 2Cor 5:21. **You rose with Me. Your new life too, has no trace of sin in it. So now, the very same Divine Life that is in Me, is flowing through you. I am the vine, you are a unique branch,** John 15:5.)

What does this mean for us?

2Cor 5:17	Therefore, if anyone is in Christ, he is a new creation; old things have passed away; behold, <u>all things have become new</u>.
Ez 36:26	'I <u>will give you a new heart</u> and put a new spirit within you; I will take the heart of stone out of your flesh and give you a heart of flesh.' **I now am a new species, a creative being of faith, energized by a new heart of love.** (It is now 'natural' for your life to express this. Anything else, living like an ordinary human being

no longer satisfies. Any trace of that old selfish life is seen as distinctly alien, foreign, dysfunctional.)

Gen 12:2   {To Abraham} ". . . I will bless you and make your name great; and <u>you shall be a blessing</u>"

Acts 20:35   . . . He {Jesus} said, "It is more blessed to give than to receive."

1Cor 15:45   Thus it is written, The first man Adam became a living being (an individual personality); the last Adam (Christ) became a **life-giving Spirit**' [restoring the dead to life]. AMP

I am a life giving Spirit—born of God, a life giving spirit so I am a life-giving Spirit

(When born again you were cut off from the ordinary Adamic race, to be born of Me a life-giver—so you are a life-giver. I made man to release life, to be a blessing which is the greatest joy of Zion Luke 10:21. You are life, so it is natural to be a life-giver. <u>If satisfied with just being blessed you miss out on the so much more I have for you.</u>)

c) **Dominion restored**

Jesus rose from the dead, having defeated the enemy. He took from Satan the keys of Death and Hades, Rev 1:18. He now had <u>all authority</u> in heaven and on earth, Matt 28:18. That very same authority He gave to us, Luke 10:19, and the right to use His name, so that we could continue His work. A policeman is given authority which he is expected to use. The authority we have been given is far far greater than that of a policeman. If we are to live as Jesus, it is essential that we use it, as He did when on earth. For this purpose the son of God was manifested, to <u>destroy</u> the works of the devil, 1 John 3:8.

There are two words in the Greek which are translated as <u>destroy</u>. 'Kalarges' is used in Heb 2:14, 'that through death He might <u>destroy</u> him who had the power of death, that is, the devil'. It means that the enemy is paralysed, impotent (for every born again believer <u>who knows this</u>). He has been disarmed, Col 2:15. His only weapon is his voice. The other word is 'luo', as used in 1John 3:8. It means that the enemy has no legal authority over us, no right to touch us (assuming our hearts and lives are focused on Him), as '<u>He has delivered us</u> from the power of darkness and conveyed us into the kingdom of the Son of His love, Col 1:13.

Give no access to the enemy

The enemy wants to destroy our relationship with God, to take our eyes off Him and onto ourselves, so he can be our master again. There are essentially three ways we give access to him. If we know them we can be vigilant and give him no place. Firstly if we <u>listen to his lies,</u> which are the negatives contradicting the Word. He uses the same strategy today as he did in the Garden of Eden, Gen 3:1-5. He wants to convey, 'God has not really got your interests at heart. He did not mean it when He said, ". . . . His Word is not true. You are better off without Him.' He wants to instil unbelief. If we respond, we feel separate, and so expose ourselves to <u>fear</u>, a major device of Satan. We must make a decision to trust Almighty God, to be unmovable, and to refuse to fear. Secondly if our <u>words</u> agree with his lies, as there is life and death in our words, Prov 18:21. If we say 'I have the flu', we give permission for it to come into our bodies. If though our words agree with the Word of God he has no access. As we declare 'we are healed', and use our authority to tell any symptom to go, it has to go. Thirdly, <u>if we sin</u> we open the door to him. Praise God, His blood was shed for us. As we ask forgiveness we are immediately cleansed.

There is no need to fight the enemy. He has been defeated. He is now under our feet, 1Cor 15:27. It is called a <u>good fight of faith</u> 1Tim 6;12. ('good' because we always win). He can throw negative thoughts at us. But, God has given us 'the shield of faith with which you will be able to <u>quench all the fiery darts</u> of the wicked one', Eph 6:16. For we walk by faith and not by sight, 2Cor 5:7. Thus, the enemy ceases to be something we fear, but becomes our 'bread' Num 14:9, knowing every challenge will bring a new victory.

Gen 1:26	Then God said," Let Us make man in Our image, according to Our likeness; <u>let them have dominion</u> over the fish of the sea, over the birds of the air, ...
Matt 28:18	. . . "All authority has been given to Me in heaven and on earth."
1John 3:8	For this purpose the Son of God was manifested, that He might destroy the works of the devil. **I know that the authority lost at the fall was restored to Jesus** **(This is not relative authority limited to specific areas, like a teacher to a class. It is perfect absolute authority over all, that at the name of Jesus, every knee has to bow,** Phil 2:10.**)**

Luke 10:19	"Behold, <u>I give **you** the authority</u> to trample on serpents and scorpions, and over all the power of the enemy, and nothing shall by any means hurt you."

> --- that same dominion has been legally restored to us, the sons of God

(You no longer live in the realm of weakness but of power; as I did, changing circumstances, healing the sick etc.)

Luke 4:18	The Spirit of the LORD is upon Me, because He has anointed Me to preach the gospel to the poor; He has sent Me to heal the brokenhearted, to proclaim liberty to the captives and recovery of sight to the blind, to set at liberty those who are oppressed.
1John 2:27	But the anointing which you have received from Him abides in you . . .
Matt 10:7-8	"And as you go, preach, saying, 'The kingdom of heaven is at hand.' Heal the sick, cleanse the lepers, raise the dead, cast out demons . . . ."

The same anointing that was on Jesus is on me to do just as He did.

(Know you have the same Spirit in you; the same heart of love burning within and the same power and authority. Use it, wherever you go setting the standards of the kingdom of God.)

d) <u>Hidden in Him</u>

Heb 10:7	Then I said, 'Behold I have come—in the volume of the book it is written of Me—to do Your will, O God.'
Eph 2:10	For we are His workmanship, created in Christ Jesus for good works, which God prepared beforehand that we should walk in them.

I know that just as God had prepared a plan for Jesus, He has for me.

(Know you will only be truly fulfilled as you delight in it and live in it.)

Ps 91:1	He who dwells in the secret place of the Most High shall abide under the shadow of the Almighty.
Col 3:3	For you died and your life is <u>hidden with Christ in God</u>. {—hallelujah!!!!!!}

Although I live in a physical body, as before I was born, I am once again hidden 'in Him'.

(Now you can live as if tucked into My glorious life of love, faith, dominion, creative power etc: It is so beautiful—you were hidden in Me in the beginning. The difference is that before, I took all the initiative. Now it is your continual choice. You can listen to the enemy or the flesh and go your own way. Or you can demonstrate your love for Me, by saying 'Yes' to Me, from deep within—full of joy and expectation. And you will discover for yourself the glory of living 'hidden in Me', and fulfil the Divine purpose I have prepared for you.)

Rom 8:29	For whom He foreknew, He also predestined to be conformed to the image of His Son, that He might be the <u>firstborn among many brethren</u>.
1John 2:6	He who says he abides in Him ought himself also to <u>walk just as He walked</u>.
John 17:18	<u>Just as</u> You sent Me into the world, I also have sent them into the world, AMP.
John 21:25	And there are also many other things that Jesus did, which if they were written one by one, I suppose that even the world itself could not contain the books that would be written. Amen.

My life is as Jesus—

(—a manifestation of the glorious Divine resurrection life, of a life giving spirit—restoring the dead to life, setting the captives free . . .)

3

IN HIM—IN HIS SOUL—IN THE WORD

The Almighty, perfect, infinite, measureless God became the Word. So the Word is the Almighty God in 'living Word' form! It (He) too is perfect, limitless!!!!! We are born of the Word, to become as the Word. Our spirits have been made by God so we can digest the Word (Him) in all His limitless qualities. 'His divine power <u>has given to us all things</u> that pertain to life and godliness, through the knowledge of Him who called us by glory and virtue, by which <u>have been given to us exceedingly great and precious promises, that through these you may be partakers of the divine nature</u>, 2Pet 1:3-4. Through the living Word His fathomless truths can become alive within, take possession of us, till our lives become an epistle, 2Cor 3:2-3, a manifestation of Him, of His love, glory and power. There is so much more . . . . As <u>we behold in the Word of God as in a</u> <u>mirror the glory of the Lord</u>, we are transformed into the same image from glory to glory, 2Cor 3:18. So it is fundamental our spirit understands and indeed celebrates the nature or dynamics of the Living Word.

Greek words throw light on the meaning of 'knowing' our Lord Looking at some of the **Greek words** which have been translated simply as 'know', reveal exciting dynamics. For example 'eido' refers to a knowledge, often used by Jesus when speaking of His knowledge of His Father like, 'I know that You always hear Me, John 11:42. It is an absolute knowledge requiring no further revelation, but an inner awareness of its absolute truth. It is used of us too; eg: John says, 'These things I have written to you who believe in the name of the Son of God, that you may <u>know</u> (eido) that you have eternal life, . . .' 1John 5:13. Paul takes it even further, a knowledge that is a fusion with Jesus, with the Word, a oneness. Is this possible? We can only understand the truth of God with the assistance of the Holy Spirit. Such a knowledge is referred to as 'ginosko' knowledge, 1Cor 2:14. He uses a more extreme form of the same word, 'epiginoskso' 1 Tim 4:3, which is not only greater knowledge, but a participation in that knowledge, for us in the Living Word, as if our spirit is dancing with His spirit in the Word, as He reveals mysteries of the truth. Or as we do the word; as we pray, heal the sick etc: Even more, it is <u>a knowledge "which perfectly unites the subject with the object."</u> We can be so yielded into a truth; we become an expression of it, an epistle! The more we see and understand its supernatural dimensions, and know them as the Greek words for 'know' suggest, the more our lives can demonstrate those dimensions . . . . !

a) <u>What/Who is this Living Word?</u>

Our awesome God is the awesome Living Word

Ps 111:10	The fear of the Lord is the beginning of wisdom;
Is 11:3	<u>His delight is in the fear of the LORD</u>, and He shall not judge by the sight of His eyes, nor decide by the hearing of His ears;
	I see, know, and delight in the awesome power, Presence, glory of our God
	(that I AM a million times greater than natural man.)
Is 66:2	. . . on this one will I look . . . who <u>trembles at My word</u>."
Ps 119:161-162	. . . <u>my heart stands in awe of Your word</u>. I rejoice at Your word, as one who finds great treasure.
	I am so conscious of You, Your glory, Presence, Spirit, permeating the word,
	(My very heart beat is inherent within it.)
2Cor 3:18	But we all, with unveiled faces, beholding {in the Word of God} as in a mirror the glory of the Lord, are being transformed into the same image from glory to glory, just as by the Spirit of the Lord.

2Cor 3:10 ... what once had splendour [the glory of the Law in the face of Moses] has come to have no splendour at all, because of the overwhelming glory that exceeds and excels it [the glory of the Gospel in the face of Jesus Christ] AMP.
Hallelujah—Your truths radiating, shining with Your glory!
(There is so much more for you to see, to embrace, to know; then you will, 'so shine' . . . . Math 5:16!)

The Word is alive

John 6:63 It is the <u>Spirit who gives life</u>; the flesh profits nothing. The <u>words that I speak</u> to you <u>are spirit, and they are life.</u>
—<u>it is alive</u>—hallelujah!
(just as I AM alive.)

John 1:14 And the <u>Word</u> became flesh and dwelt among us, and we beheld His glory, the glory as of the only begotten of the Father, full of grace and truth.
I delight in the <u>Living</u> Word
(—as you love Me, delight in Me, love the Living Word and delight in it.)

Heb 4:12 For the <u>word of God is living and powerful</u>, and sharper than any two-edged sword, piercing even to the division of soul and spirit, and of joints and marrow, and is a discerner of the thoughts and intents of the heart. And there is no creature hidden from <u>His sight</u>, but all things are naked and open to the <u>eyes of Him</u> to whom we must give account. {The Word sees with eyes of love, reveals, analyzes.}

Acts 19:20 So the word of the Lord grew mightily and prevailed.
Inherent within the Living Word is all the power, Presence and personality of God
(The same power is released as when I said, "Let there be light" and there was light. Gen 1:3 Know too, it is an expression of all that I {Jesus} am, My glory, anointing, plus all My character—My love, zeal, faith etc: As you realise this, every truth becomes <u>so much more</u>, an expression of My love—of our relationship.

Eg: You are healed because I love you. You are certain of it because of My faithfulness . . . .)

The Word is outside time

John 1:1-2	In the beginning was the Word, and the Word was with God, and the Word was God. He was in the beginning with God.
John 8:58	Jesus said to them, "Most assuredly, I say to you, <u>before Abraham was, I AM</u>."
Heb 13:8	Jesus Christ is the same yesterday, today and forever.

I delight in the Word being outside time
(My Presence, anointing in the Word is alive, fresh — now — in the present; I AM . . . . For a season I entered into time, but was not bound by it.)

Is 41:4	"Who has performed and done it, calling the generations from the beginning? I the LORD, am the first; and with the last I am He."
Rev 22:13	"I am the Alpha and the Omega, the First and the Last (the Before all and the end of all)." AMP

I was in You (Almighty God) in the beginning and will be at the end
(Let such knowledge give you a deep security in Me. Like Jesus, you have entered time for a season.)

Gen 17:5	". . . . I <u>have made you</u> a father of many nations." {At the time Abraham had no child.}
1Pet 2:24 —	by whose stripes <u>you were healed.</u>
Col 1:13	He <u>has delivered us</u> from the power of darkness and conveyed us into the kingdom of the Son of His love.

Hallelujah — as a new creation, I was healed 2000 years ago, delivered, made a king, Rev 1:6, etc:
(<u>I have already done it for you</u>. This is the truth, reality — delight in it, and live it.)

Rom 4:17	. . . God, who . . . calls those things which do not exist as though they did.

Heb 11:1   Now faith is the substance of things hoped for, the evidence of things not seen.
Mark 11:24   Therefore I say to you, whatever things you ask <u>when you pray</u>, believe that you receive them, and you will have them.
When I pray I know it is <u>done in the spirit</u>. The future has been brought into the present.
(Irrespective of how you feel, you have received it. It is done. So speak it, rejoice in it, and the circumstance will have to change, Rom 4:20.)

The Word is perfect

Ps 12:6   The words of the Lord are <u>pure words</u>, like silver tried in a furnace of earth, purified seven times.
James 1:25   But he who looks into the <u>perfect law of liberty</u> and continues in it, and is not a forgetful hearer but a doer of the work, this one will be blessed in what he does.
John 14:27   Peace I leave with you, <u>My peace I give to you; not as the world gives do I give to you</u>.
Let not your heart be troubled, neither let it be afraid.
I delight in the Word being perfect, it's absolute purity; You are absolute truth—perfect love, perfect faith, perfect freedom . . .
(The Word is, was before time began. My truths are unpolluted by carnal relativity—no trace of dust. Eg: The 'world' thinks of 'freedom' as from a past bondage or addiction, but with My freedom no bondage is possible. Re 'authority', we think of it with our family or a policeman in his area, but with Me it is absolute authority over all! <u>The more you see and understand My perfection the more you can get to know Me as I AM.</u>)

b) <u>Fertile ground for this awesome Living Word!</u>

i) Let the Holy Spirit be in control

The Holy Spirit is our teacher, John 14:26, Who enables us to understand a truth. We can ask Him to teach us as we meditate on the Word, Ps 119:18. When listening to a message, ask Him to quicken a truth. He will and it will come alive. This is God speaking to you, today. As we continue to meditate on that specific truth, to chew it and act on it, God delights to intervene.

But there is much more. Do we want the living Word to permeate our whole being? In the Old Testament Ezekiel prophesied a dynamic, abhorrent to fallen independent man, but glorious to us. 'I will put My Spirit within you and <u>cause you</u> to walk in My statutes, Ez 36:27. Paul refers to the same when he says, '<u>it is God Who works in you both to will and to do for His good pleasure</u>, Phil 2:13. Hallelujah—our desires, thoughts and actions are no longer our own, but are initiated by the Holy Spirit. I remember when I first came across these scriptures, they seemed so distasteful. Although I had given my heart to God I still wanted to be the one in control of my life, so He would appreciate my efforts! It was not until I started truly celebrating the death of my old life with all its independence, pride etc: that I was able to see the glory of such scriptures. That Almighty God's heart had replaced mine, Ez 36:26, so I could rest dependent Him; on His glorious perfect love burning within me, which is infinitely superior to my old heart. <u>How much better than me possessing the Holy Spirit, to be possessed by the Holy Spirit,—by Almighty God, truly hidden in Him,</u> Col 3:3.

Success in the Kingdom of God

It is interesting that in the world, the higher, the more successful you are, the more you might expect to be in control. In the Kingdom of God it is the opposite. Paul saw himself as a bondservant, a slave. Jesus never did or spoke anything other than that directed by His Father. Yet this is the way of true fulfilment. Jesus had more joy than all His companions, Heb 1:9. It is the same for us. In His Presence is fullness of joy, Ps 16:11. I remember before going to Bible School, God gave me three words, the '<u>glory</u> of a <u>love slave</u>'. The more we truly yield our hearts to Him with joy, the more our lives can be swallowed up by His. The more we delight in Him possessing us, the more we can be one with Him, fused with Him. So that, 'in Him we live, and move, and have our being,' Acts 17:28.

John 14:26   But the Helper, the Holy Spirit, whom the Father will send in My name, <u>He will teach you all things</u>, . . .
John 16:13   However, when He, the Spirit of truth, has come, He will guide you into all truth; for He will not speak on His own

	authority, but whatever He hears He will speak; and He will tell you things to come.
Rom 8:16	The Spirit Himself bears witness with our spirit that we are children of God,
	It is too marvellous that I have You, Holy Spirit as my own personal teacher
	(The external law 'the ministry of death', was glorious. It has been replaced by the ministry of the Spirit from within, which is infinitely more glorious, 2Cor 3:7-8.)
Ps 37:4	Delight yourself also in the LORD, and <u>He shall give you the desires of your heart</u>.
Ps 36:8	They are abundantly satisfied with the fullness of Your house, and You give them drink from <u>the river of Your pleasures</u>. For with You is the fountain of life;
	What a joy that my heart is beating with Yours
	(Know that My joys are the real joys. The joys that the world offers are as a shadow compared to what I have to give you.)
Ez 36:27	I will put My Spirit within you and cause you to walk in My statutes, and you will keep My judgments and do them.
Phil 2:13	For it is God who works in you both to will and to do for His good pleasure.
2Cor 5:14	For the love of Christ compels us,
	Hallelujah—the Holy Spirit teaches, guides, motivates me.
	(My beloved you are swallowed up in life, 2Cor 5:4.)

ii) <u>Our heart—'Yes Lord' with joy!</u>

We may be doing all the correct things, but miss out on the vital glorious union, the inexpressible joy He longs for us to experience daily, 1Pet 1:8-9. He said to such a church in Ephesus, "Nevertheless I have this against you, that you have left your first love." Rev 2:4. God wants a heart that is alive, burning with His zeal. One that has no other agenda polluting it (status, healing, prosperity etc:). Such a heart not only receives the living Word with joy, but also **<u>with joy does whatever He prompts us to do</u>**, Ps 40:8. Why?—Because we know that whatever He asks of us will be for our good, Rom 8:28. We even count the trials as a joy, James 1:2, because we know He loves us perfectly, 1 John 4:18. We have been set free from fear. Not only because the old person we used to be, full of fear, was crucified with Him, but because He is our security, not man or circumstances. We know we are His workmanship, His work of art; He is moulding us, Eph 2:10. The joy of the Lord is our strength, Neh 8:10. This joy is so important to God. We see it even in the Old Testament. One of the reasons for the curse coming on the children of Israel was, 'Because you did not serve the LORD your God with joy and gladness of heart, . . . Deut 28:47. We are commanded to 'Rejoice in the Lord always.' Phil 4:4. **God does not want a people who obey because they have to, but a people who delight in doing whatever they are asked**. He can then delight in us, 'He will rejoice over you with singing,' Zeph 3:17. <u>Throughout the sacred Scriptures great emphasis is placed on the **heart**</u>.

Praise God!

It does not require degrees, a good education or being in a good job to be used in extraordinary ways by God. He delights to choose nobodies. Gideon belonged to the weakest clan and he was the least in his father's house, Judges 6:15. David was just a shepherd boy, but God saw His heart. 'The LORD has sought for Himself <u>a man after His own heart'</u>, 1Sam 13:14. and made him king. What about you? Nothing is impossible for our God, and we are in Him!

Our new heart

Ez 36:26 I will give you a new heart and put a new spirit within you.

Deut 30:6 And the LORD your God will circumcise your heart, . . . to love the LORD your God with all your heart and with all your soul, that you may live.
Thank You that you have given me a new heart so it is my joy to love You
(The Christian life is so simple, just to love Me with all your heart and others with the same love. As you put Me first, I abundantly deal with all else, Matt 6:33.)

Rev 2:4 Nevertheless I have this against you, that you have left your first love.
Forgive me Lord. I see, it is so beautiful. You long for me to be in love with You.

With joy I will say 'Yes' to whatever You ask of me . . . .
(Yes, my beloved, be in love with Me and you will come to know how much I am in love with you.)

Jer 15:16 <u>Your words were found, and I ate them, and Your word was to me the joy and rejoicing of my heart;</u>

Col 3:16 Let the word of Christ dwell in you richly in all wisdom, teaching and admonishing one another in psalms and hymns and spiritual songs, singing with grace in your hearts to the Lord.
I treasure Your Word as I treasure You
(so I can reveal more and more of the depths of the glory of My Living Word.)

1Pet 1:8 {Jesus} whom having not seen you love. Though now you do not see Him, yet believing, you **rejoice with joy inexpressible** and full of glory,

Eph 3:19 to know the love of Christ, which far surpasses mere knowledge; that you may be filled [through all your being] unto all the fullness of God [may have the richest measure of the divine Presence, and become a body wholly filled and flooded with God Himself]! AMP
Thank you Lord 'joy inexpressible' is becoming more and more my experience
(Throughout your Christian life as you say 'Yes' to Me wholeheartedly you are beautiful in My eyes, and I can open heaven for you.)

Neh 8:10 . . . the joy of the Lord is your strength.
Ps 40:8 I delight to do Your will, O my God,
Is 12:3 . . . with joy your will draw water from the wells of salvation.
Phil 4:4 Rejoice in the Lord always. Again I will say, rejoice!
Hallelujah—this is the life in Zion! Phil 3:20
(As you continually rejoice in Me, you are focussed on Me, your confidence is in Me, which means I can so easily give you My thoughts and intervene.)

James 1:2   My brethren, count it all joy when you fall into various trials,
Rom 8:28   And we know all things work together for good to those who love God,
My security is in You, not in man or circumstances
(My beloved know that the <u>genuineness</u> of your faith, is <u>much more precious</u> to Me than gold that perishes, 1Pet 1:7. It is an expression of your trust in Me.)

Matt 5:8   <u>Blessed are the pure in heart,</u> for they shall see God.
Prov 4:21-23   Keep {guard} them {My Words} in the midst of your heart, for they are life to those who find them, and health to all their flesh. <u>Keep {guard} your heart with all diligence</u>, for out of it spring the issues of life.
You are my all in all
(Like the crown jewels are treasured and guarded, so treasure and guard your heart.)

John 7:38   "He who believes in Me, as the Scripture has said, <u>out of his heart</u> will flow rivers of living water."
Ez 47:9   And it shall be that every living thing that moves, wherever the rivers go, will live.
Every day I will be a blessing, miracles will flow.
(and the words you speak are as Mine; they are spirit and they are life, John 6:63.)

c) <u>Receive your miracle, — step into the glory of the Word</u>

But <u>be doers of the word</u>, and not hearers only, deceiving yourselves, James 1:22. Faith without works is dead, James 2:20.

God wants us to approach the Word of God in a way totally different from which it was approached in the days of the Old Testament. unfortunately many churches still operate with an Old Testament mindset. The glory is that we do not have to obey as in the Old Testament. That was the means for man who was separated from God to acquire the blessings of the covenant. That covenant is now obsolete, Heb 8:13. We are part of a better covenant, Heb 7:22. God has made us new creations, 2Cor 5:17. We are not separate from Him, John 15:5. The Kingdom of God is within us, Luke 17:21. The blessings are already ours, Eph 1:3. As we look into the glory of Word of God as a mirror, 2Cor 3:18, we discover what we are and how God wants us to live. **We believe it and <u>delight to do it</u>**; see the power and glory of the Living Word, and <u>with joy act on the basis that it is so</u>. If someone gave you an iron, there would be no point in continuing to ask for one, or to leave it in its box. You simply discover how the iron works from the instructions, <u>**do**</u> what is required and it will operate correctly. <u>With joy</u>, you know that when you switch it on it will work. We do not need to ask God for love or His anointing because it has already been given us, Rom 5:5, 1John 2:20,27. When ministering we are excited, full of anticipation, because we expect it to operate. We may pray, 'Lord let my heart be burning with Your love today, let the anointing be so evident today', and it will be. As we act, trusting in a specific truth, we know the Holy Spirit within delights to confirm it, Mark 16:20.

Knowing the power of the life inherent in the Living Word

God chose to make all His power, the power of Almighty God, to be channelled through words. When He said, 'Let there be light', Gen 1:3, all His power was activated in those four words to make light in all its perfection. When Jesus said to a man in the synagogue with a withered hand, 'Stretch out your hand', Mark 3:5, all the power of God was in those four words. As he acted and stretched out his arm, all the power required to make it do so was released! Oh the power of the words of Jesus! When He said to a dead boy, 'Young man . . . arise,' Luke 7:14, the power in those words was such that even his spirit had to return to his body, and the young man sat up and spoke.

"Come"

The event of Jesus walking on the water has spoken so much to me. One day Jesus sent the disciples off in a boat, Matt 14:22. A storm arose. At about 3.00 am Jesus walked towards them on the water. The disciples were terrified thinking it was a ghost. Jesus assured them it was He. Peter said, 'If it is You, ask me to come to You. Jesus said, 'Come'. Now in that one word, 'Come' was all the power of Almighty God to enable the water to hold the weight of Peter. I am sure God would have loved it if all the disciples had got out of the boat and had a party on the water. Only Peter responded. Yes, he sank when he took his eyes off Jesus, but Jesus immediately took his hand and surely walked with him back to the boat. Every promise in the Bible is like 'Come'. In it is all the power of God for it to become a reality. We know that every truth was established before time began, John1:1. Each is pure indeed perfect, Ps 12:6; perfect freedom, perfect healing, perfect authority etc, has been provided for us. Yet in this story, only Peter responded to the word 'Come'. Most Christians are like the other disciples in the boat. They were doing what they had been instructed to do, going to the other side, being good Christians. They hear a promise, 'You are healed, 'You are free', 'You have the same anointing as Jesus had when on earth', and respond, 'Yes, very interesting', but they stay in the boat. Not realising that that <u>every promise is there for them, but it is activated as they believe it and step out of the boat</u>, act on it. A paralyzed man was let down through the roof to come into Jesus' Presence. Jesus did not look at the mess it must have made. The bible records His reaction. It only mentions, '<u>He saw their faith</u>', Luke 5:20. They believed. He said to the paralyzed man, 'arise, take up your bed, . . .' In those words was all the power of God required for him to do it. Immediately he rose up before them, took up what he had been lying on, and departed to his own house, glorifying God, Luke 5:24-25. The Words of Jesus are just as alive today. Has your faith been stirred as you have been 'hearing' these truths? Has faith been rising?

"Yes Lord"

I have seen thousands healed as they believe the truth that they are healed Is 53:4-5, 1Pet 2:24, indeed, that they were healed two thousand years ago. Despite the symptom still being very apparent, they realise that the Word of God—God, is far greater than anything in the natural which He made. They believe. I get them to start praising God for their healing, then to rise up to their feet and start dancing, declaring they are healed. As they act, as they start dancing, their miracle happens. There have been so many testimonies, very serious cancer tumours have disappeared, the paralysed walk, the blind see, etc.

If a stranger asked you to do something, it would be right for you to be reticent. But when Almighty God, the Maker of the heavens and the earth, Who loves you perfectly says, 'Come, trust Me' how can you not but say, 'Yes' and with joy step out of the boat trusting Him. Right now why don't you expect a miracle? Thank Him that you are healed or free from that addiction. Hear Him, Almighty God saying to you, 'Rise up'. In those two words is all the power of God to accomplish your miracle. Immediately, jump up from your seat or bed with joy in your spirit, declaring you are healed, free—hallelujah! As you do, the Holy Spirit will make sure the miracle is yours!

d) Other ways our spirits can touch and embrace the glory of the Word

Like an electric current

Heb 1:3 who being the brightness of His glory and the express image of His person, and <u>upholding all things by the word of His power</u>, . . .
I delight that all things are now being held together by Him, by the Living Word
(When I spoke it is as if an electric current was released, which is just as alive now. As your spirit sees this and says "Yes", it is as if all My love, glory and power inherent within a particular truth, healing, peace etc, is activated. As if you have raised a divine wire making contact, so it can flow directly into you!) — hallelujah!

Intimacy

2Cor 3:18 But we all, with unveiled face, beholding {in the Word of God} as in a mirror the glory of the Lord, are being transformed into the same image from glory to glory, just as by the Spirit of the Lord.

Song 1:2 Let him kiss me with the kisses of his mouth—for your love is better than wine.

John 4:24 God is Spirit and those who worship Him must worship in spirit and truth. {Worship in Greek is 'proskuneo', pros meaning 'toward' and 'kuneo' to kiss.}
Kissing the Word and being kissed by the Word
(Embracing the essence of My glory in that truth. As you abandon yourself to its unfathomable mysteries, that very glory will permeate your whole being. O, let Me, that truth kiss you, embrace you.)

Song 5:1	I have come to my garden, my sister, my spouse; I have gathered my myrrh with my spice; I have eaten my honeycomb with my honey; I have drunk my wine with my milk.

As I delight in You, the Living Word, so You delight in Me!

(Like an insect feasting in the glory of a flower, delighting in its colour, fragrance, delight in Me, the living Word, feasting on its extraordinary delights. In it is all My love—glory! being outside time—glory!, its perfection—glory. Know I delight in the beauty of those same things I am fashioning in you!)

Ps 119:130	The entrance of Your words gives light; it gives understanding to the simple.
Heb 3:6	... we hold fast and firm to the end our <u>joyful and exultant confidence and sense of triumph</u> in our hope [in Christ]. AMP

—conception, pregnancy and birth
(You know in reality, in the spirit, it is already done; it is yours now, so rejoice as the outcome is inevitable.)

Ignited

Jer 15:16	Your words were found, and I ate them, and Your word was to me the joy and rejoicing of my heart;
Jer 23:29	"Is not My word like a fire?" says the LORD, "and like a hammer that breaks the rock in pieces?"
Jer 20:9	But His word was in my heart like a burning fire shut up in my bones; I was weary of holding it back, and I could not.

The glory of the Word can energize my whole being

(As you feast on a truth, Divine exuberant joy or even a burning fire can erupt from deep within.

Decision to be unmovable

Prov 23:7   For as he thinks in his heart, so is he.

Josh 1:8   This Book of the Law shall not depart from <u>your mouth</u>, but you shall <u>meditate in it day and night</u>, that you may observe to do according to all that is written in it. For then you will make your way prosperous, and <u>then you will have good success</u>.
I will focus only on the glorious truth
(As you meditate and speak the Word, it not only builds up your faith. It also creates . . . .)

Ps 125:1   Those who trust in the LORD are like Mount Zion, which cannot be moved but abides forever.

2Cor 10:4-5   For the weapons of our warfare are not carnal but mighty in God for pulling down strongholds, casting down arguments and every high thing that exalts itself against the knowledge of God, bringing every thought into captivity to the obedience of Christ,

Rom 8:13   For if you live according to the flesh you shall die; but if by the Spirit you put to death {mortify} the deeds of the body, you will live.
I will not tolerate any contrary thoughts or even emotions—
(If fear, pride, lust, anger etc: arise, do not fight them. That is carnal and bound to fail. You know it is a lie as the old life is dead. <u>Just close the door</u>, give them no place, and declare the truth you are loved perfectly, free . . . . <u>Then I can transform</u> that which used to dissipate your energy into divine energy. Thus, it will be used to further kindle the fire of My love burning in you.)

As Jesus was the Living Word, so are we

1Pet 1:23   Having been born again, not of corruptible seed but incorruptible, through the word of God which lives and abides forever,

2Cor 3:2-3	You are our epistle written in our hearts, known and read by all men; clearly you are an epistle of Christ, ministered by us, written not with ink but by the Spirit of the living God, not on tablets of stone but on tablets of flesh, that is, of the heart. **As You, when on earth, were an expression of the Living Word of God, so am I** **(A dog gives birth to a dog, a cat to a cat, so the <u>perfect incorruptible Living Word</u> has given birth to the perfect incorruptible Living Word, which is you!)**
Is 60:1	Arise, shine; for your light has come! And the glory of the LORD is risen upon you.
John 17:22	And <u>the glory which You gave Me I have given them, that they may be one **just as** We are one</u>. **(You have received My glory so . . .)**

I am one with Jesus, the Living Word, <u>just as</u> He was one with His Father

4

IN HIM — IN HIS SPIRIT

a) Aware of the dynamic of His spirit in the created world

A person may be ugly, or old and wizened in the natural, but if they are filled with the spirit, one can sense or even see the glory of God in them. In the same way a tree, a house, a room, irrespective of its natural qualities, beauty, or ugliness, can exude a peace or an unease. This is because, all things are upheld by Him, by the Word of His power, Heb 1:3. In all things there is an aspect of the life of the Spirit of God which is sustaining them. It is this which enables things to respond to Him; trees, storms, diseases, crippled bodies heard Him and had to obey, Matt 17:5. We are as He is, so things hear and obey us!!! Nature, even mountains, have been commanded to rejoice, Ps 148:7-10, which they do unless quenched by man. There was an experiment in which a man had two trees growing by his window. To one, he expressed disgust and contempt. He told it that it was ugly, that it would never do any good. To the other love, that it was beautiful, that it would bear excellent fruit. In six weeks the tree that had received negative, destructive vibes had withered, indeed it was almost dead, but the other tree was flourishing. Creation responds to our spirits, to what we do and say.

Also God delights to reveal Himself through things; to speak to us of His glory, His nature, Rom 1:20. He spoke to Jeremiah through a pot in a potter's house, Jer 18:2-11. He longs to do this with each one of us. He is speaking to us all the time, as He was with Jesus, who was continually prompted by His Father, John 5:19. This is what abiding in Him means, the vital union of John 15:5. For example, as eating cereal, I may notice the way the milk unites all the different ingredients, and the thought arises, it is like the way His Spirit unites us perfectly. I may see a puddle reflecting the sun, and a thought arises, this is how we can reflect Him. Or a scripture may rise up from within, that living water is flowing from us, John 7:38. This can happen for each of us more and more, if we are aware that things can speak to us and are <u>expectant that He will speak though them</u>.

He is in all things

Col 1:16-17   For <u>by Him all things were created</u> that are in heaven and that are on earth, visible and invisible, whether thrones or dominions or principalities or powers. All things were created <u>through Him and for Him</u>. And He is before all things, and <u>in Him all things consist</u>.

Is 6:3   And one cried to another and said: "Holy, holy, holy is the LORD of hosts; <u>the whole earth is full of His glory</u>!"
I see Him, His spirit in all things
(Delight in My Presence always, you are never alone.
Know the spirit in them delights in your presence!)—
hallelujah!

Ps 19:1-4   The heavens declare the glory of God; and the firmament shows His handiwork. Day unto day <u>utters speech,</u> and night unto night <u>reveals knowledge</u>. There is no speech nor language where <u>their voice is not heard</u>. Their line has gone out through all the earth, and <u>their words</u> to the end of the world.
      —things speak and reveal knowledge
(They possess hidden secrets and they will speak to you <u>if</u>
<u>you are expectant</u>—of My beauty, perfection wisdom etc:
You may see a stone and be reminded you are a living
stone, 1Pet 2:5 . . .)

Ps 148:7-10   Praise the Lord from the earth . . . mountains and all hills; fruitful trees and all cedars; beasts and all cattle; creeping things and flying fowl;

Ps 96:1, 9   . . . . Sing to the LORD, all the earth . . . . Tremble before Him, all the earth.

Ps 96:12   Let the field be joyful, and all that is in it. Then all the trees of the woods will rejoice before the Lord.
      —things praise Him and rejoice

(Which is why you find it easier to worship in open country—they are already rejoicing.)

Ez 37:4 . . . He said to me, "Prophecy to these bones, and say to them, 'O dry bones **hear** {listen attentively} the word of the LORD!'"

Matt 17:20 ". . . for assuredly, I say to you, if you have faith as a mustard seed, you will say to this mountain, 'Move from here to there,' and it will move; and nothing will be impossible for you."
—things hear and obey
(This is the Divine order—use the dominion I have given you.)

Rom 8:19-21 For the earnest expectation of the creation eagerly waits for the revealing of the sons of God . . . because the creation itself also will be delivered from the bondage of corruption into the glorious liberty of the children of God.
—things long to be liberated
(Elements of creation have been quenched, subdued, perverted—for you to liberate!)

b) In His Spirit manifest in His breath, wind

In both Old and New Testaments the word used for spirit can Be translated as wind or breath. The context decides which. It is essentially His spirit in the form of breath or wind. It is so beautiful that His breath is an expression of His Spirit and His Words were created by His breath. The scriptures reveal how His breath and wind carries life and power. As He is, so are we . . . .

Gen 2:7 And the LORD God formed man of the dust of the ground, and breathed into his nostrils the breath of life {spirit}; and man became a living being.
Through Your breath you imparted life—
(Thus, man received a spirit enabling him to relate to Me. You were in Me as I did this.)

In Him — so much MORE!

Ex 14:21   Then Moses stretched out his hand over the sea; and <u>the LORD caused the sea to go back by a strong east wind</u> {spirit} all that night, and made the sea into dry land, and the waters were divided.
I see its power when manifest as wind
(My breath/wind can change any circumstance.)

Num 11:31   Now <u>a wind {spirit} went out from the LORD</u>, and it brought quail from the sea and left them fluttering near the camp, . . .

Ps 78:27   He also rained meat on them like the dust, feathered fowl like the sand of the seas;
    — It has power to create
(My first act was to create, to create the heavens and the earth, Gen 1:1. It is My nature and joy to create. You have the same life and capacity in you!)

Mark 15:37   And Jesus cried out with a loud voice, and <u>breathed His last</u>.
(My last breath as part of the Adamic race. When you were born again, your old life, with its 'natural breath' died, Rom 6:6.)

John 20:22   And when He had said this, <u>He breathed on them</u>, and said to them, "Receive the Holy Spirit {breath}".
Your breath imparted the Divine life 'zoe' life, the very essence of God
(Again you were there in Me, with Me, when I breathed the breath that produced the first new creation—a new order of being.)

Acts 2:2   And suddenly there came a sound from heaven, as of a <u>rushing mighty wind</u> {breath}, and it <u>filled the whole house</u> where they were sitting.

Acts 2:4   <u>**'and they were all filled with the Holy Spirit'**</u>
    -- the power of the Holy Spirit—as a rushing mighty wind
(An immeasurable measure of My infinite supernatural power could now reside in human bodies.)

How does this apply to us?

John 6:63	..."<u>The words that I speak</u> to you are <u>spirit</u>, and they are <u>life</u>." {life—'zoe', Divine life}
Is 55:11	"So shall My word be that goes forth from My mouth; it shall not return to Me void, but it shall accomplish what I please, and it shall prosper in the thing for which I sent it."
Prov 18:21	<u>Death and life are in the power of the tongue</u>, and those who love it will eat its fruit.

My words contain the same Divine breath/wind—they too are alive!

(Your life is now energized, guided, prompted from your spirit within, as it was with Jesus. And like Him, your words, empowered by your breath, produce whatever you speak.)

Gen 1:26	God said, Let Us [Father, Son, and Holy Spirit] make mankind in <u>Our image</u>, after <u>Our likeness</u>, and let them have <u>complete authority</u> over the fish of the sea, the birds.... AMP.
Ez 37:9	He said <u>to me</u>, "<u>Prophesy to the breath</u>, prophesy, son of man, and <u>say to the breath</u>, 'Thus says the Lord GOD "<u>Come from the four winds, O breath, and breathe on these</u> <u>slain, that they may live.</u>'"
Act 3:6	Then Peter said, "Silver and gold I do not have, but <u>what I do have</u> I give you: In the name of Jesus Christ of Nazareth, rise up and walk."

I can decree even life to enter a body!

(Be bold—you are born of a 'life giving Spirit [restoring the dead to life],' 1Cor 15:45 AMP.)

c) In His Spirit manifest as fire in us

Divine energy

When we were born again the old selfish heart of stone was removed to be replaced by one of love, Ez 36:26. When we are filled with the Spirit, we receive the power of God, Acts 1:8, but also His **fire**, Matt 3:11. That heart of love is set aflame; it starts **burning with Divine energy**. New desires take hold of us, a new zeal to set captives free; those bound and oppressed so that they can know this glorious life of Zion. It is the same motivation that brought Jesus here on earth, that drove Paul to do what he did, 'the love of Christ compels us', 2Cor 5:14. Electricity flows through wires. This is like God's sacred wire through which His Divine energy operates and miracles flow naturally, as they did in His life and those of the early church. Jesus tells us one of the reasons He came was to <u>send fire on the earth</u>, Luke 12:49. Thus when we know we have received this fire, and are aware of what it means, we can continue His work, destroying the works of the enemy, IJohn 3:8, and establishing His Kingdom on earth.

Most Christians do not expect miracles to flow through them, because of unbiblical teaching, There is a love in their heart which longs to see a particular person set free of their ailment, but they 'feel' powerless. They demonstrate love by caring for the person, yet there is a frustration within as it seems so far below the life as described in the Bible. There are two aspects of this Divine 'love' fire in the Scriptures, which if understood can rectify this.

i) An understanding of the zeal or passion of God's love.

This is very evident even in the Old Testament. One of His names is Jealous, Ex 34:14. His love is described, 'its flames are flames of fire, a most vehement flame', Song 8:6. In the Old Testament, again and again His people went their own way, but it did not change His ardent 'jealous' love for them. Jesus' life was a demonstration of love, not just in dying for us. It was evident in the way He lived. It motivated Him to <u>take extraordinary steps to ensure another's well being</u>. For example, He travelled across Samaria, where the Jews did not go, to meet a woman in great need, and set her free to become the evangelist He had ordained her to be, John 4:3-42. If we are 'in Him', the same zeal of this Divine love is burning!!! At times my body has felt tired during an excessively full schedule abroad. When I remind myself that His divine fire is burning within, that He has brought me here for this time, a fresh love for those precious people is birthed, and with it new energy!

ii) The significance of God being a consuming fire,
Heb 12:29.

In the Old Testament the Hebrew word used for 'consuming' means, to eat or devour. In the New Testament the Greek word means, to consume utterly. Jesus came to destroy the works of the enemy, 1John 3:8, and so He did wherever He went. Again and again He totally <u>healed all the sick</u> who came to Him and set the captives free. It was as if this consuming fire took the form of a Holy righteous anger <u>compelling Him to act to annihilate Satan's works</u>. We see this anger demonstrated physically when He made a whip and turned out those who were abusing the temple, 'When He had made a whip of cords, He drove them all out of the temple, with the sheep and the oxen, and poured out the changers' money and overturned the tables.' Indeed His disciples remembered that 'it was written, "Zeal for Your house has eaten Me up."' John 2:14-17. <u>Now, our bodies are the temple of the Holy Spirit</u>, 1Cor 6:19. Jesus rarely initiated a healing. Surely it was this righteous anger that <u>stirred Him into action</u> when He saw a woman suffering in the synagogue? She was bent over, unable to stand upright. He called her to Him and healed her. When the Pharisees objected He replied,
'Ought not this woman, being a daughter of Abraham, whom Satan has bound—think of it—for eighteen years, be loosed from this bond on the Sabbath?" Luke 13:16. Glory—<u>if we are in Him, we are in this righteous anger</u>—It too is part of who we are!

Commanded to 'be angry' with a righteous anger

When I discovered that we are commanded to **be angry**, it totally changed my mindset. Eph 4:26 says, '<u>Be angry</u>, and do not sin; do not
let the sun go down on your wrath.' This is normally interpreted to mean, do not be angry. But if it does happen, make up for it as soon as possible. But the tense in the Greek makes it abundantly clear that it is a command—'Be angry'. (This righteous anger is totally different from a fleshly self-centred anger. We are exhorted not to let it become such, 'do not sin'. [Sin for the new creation is responding in the flesh, rather than in faith, Rom14:23, and outside love, Gal 5:6.]) God does not want us to passively accept what the enemy has done. Was it not such an anger that rose up in David when he saw Goliath? His response was, 'Who is this uncircumcised Philistine, that he should defy the armies of the living God?', 1Sam 17:26, while the Israelite army cowered in fear. They had forgotten the covenant, so exposed themselves to the enemy's

devices. 'My people are destroyed through lack of knowledge', Hos 4:6. David knew Goliath had no right or power over God's covenanted people, Deut 28:7. No more should cancer, drug addiction, etc, have any power in the body of Christ. We are part of a better covenant. Jesus' death has set us free, Gal 5:1. As a new creation, disease, fear, oppression should be totally foreign to us. When I see people sick, something within, this Divine fire often rises up in me, as I know that sickness should have no place in His treasured children. What is this HIV or blindness that dares defy the body of Christ? It compels me to act, knowing that Almighty God's miracle power will intervene, confirming my words or actions, and He does. I have seen the lame, blind, mute, paralysed set free, plus those with terminal cancer and HIV. Our God is a million times greater than anything in this world which He made. Nothing is impossible for Him. Glory we are 'in Him'.

'Thank You Lord that this same Divine fire that was burning in You is burning in each one of us. So our lives can be flames of fire!' Heb 1:7

Luke 12:49   <u>I came to send fire on earth</u>, and how I wish it were already kindled!

Matt 3:11   I {John} indeed baptize you with water unto repentance, but He who is coming after me is mightier than I, ... <u>He will baptize you with the Holy Spirit and fire</u>.
The long awaited promise
(so you can be truly alive, not lulled to sleep by the enemy, 2Cor 4:4.)

Acts 2:3   Then there appeared to them divided tongues, as of fire, and one sat upon each of them.

2Cor 5:14   For the love of Christ compels us . . . .
My heart is on fire, energized burning with His passionate love—alive!
(It is as if a Divine battery is operating deep within you.)

What is this fire?
His Presence

Ex 3:2 — And the Angel of the LORD appeared to him in a flame of fire from the midst of a bush . . . . . the bush was burning with fire, but the bush was not consumed.
The very Presence of God, I AM spoke from the bush
(You were there too in Me. An ordinary bush with I AM in it became a supernatural bush. It did not burn. I spoke through it. You were an ordinary human being, but now I AM—My very Presence is living in you. You are a supernatural being.)

Ardent, passionate love, zeal

Ex 34:14 — for you shall worship no other god, for the LORD, <u>whose name is Jealous, is a jealous God</u> {'jealous' refers to God's passionate commitment to us, an absolute intolerance of anything that would divide our affection.}

Song 8:6-7 — For love is as strong as death, . . . <u>its flames are flames of fire, a most vehement flame.</u> Many waters cannot quench love, nor can the floods drown it.

1Pet 4:8 — And above all things have <u>fervent love</u> for one another . . . .
I love my brethren with the same fervent love with which He loves me
(This is <u>natural</u> for you, simply an expression of this burning fire, which is part of who you are.)

Righteous anger

Heb 12:29 — For our God is a consuming fire.

Ps 97:3-5 — A fire goes before Him, and burns up His enemies round about . . . The mountains melt like wax at the presence of the LORD, at the presence of the Lord of the whole earth.
The very Presence of God in me makes the enemy quake
(when you appear.)

Eph 4:26	<u>Be angry</u>, and do not sin; do not let the sun go down on your wrath,
1Sam 17:26	David spoke "... who is this uncircumcised Philistine, that he should defy the armies of the living God?"

I am commanded to let that righteous anger arise when I see the work of the enemy
(Be 'jealous' for your beloved brethren.)

John 2:15, 17	When He had made a whip of cords, He drove them all out of the temple, with the sheep and the oxen, and poured out the changers' money and overturned the tables. Then His disciples remembered that it was written, "Zeal for Your house has eaten Me up."

I have the same righteous anger that can well up in me causing me to act
(You know you are as equipped as I was when on earth so when you see a brother or sister bound, oppressed, suffering, this is your 'natural' response. You set them free as I did.)

Jer 20:9	... But His word was in my heart like a burning fire shut up in my bones; I was weary of holding it back, and I could not, ...
Heb 1:7	.... 'Who makes His angels spirits and <u>His ministers a flame of fire</u>.

We are FLAMES OF FIRE
(truly alive)

5

IN HIM—IN HIS BODY

In 1Cor 12:12-26, Paul describes being part of His body, one person being a foot another an eye stressing that each of us has been given a unique gifting which He longs to be developed. The body will not work if everyone is a foot or an eye, but together, united we represent Him! Here we are looking at 'in His body' more in terms of His actual body, when on earth and as He is now. This does not make rational sense, but I have just let the scriptures speak for themselves, and the Holy Spirit has opened my spirit to glorious dynamics. I trust He will for you too.

Bones!

2 Kings 13:21 So it was, as they were burying a man, . . . they put the man in the tomb of Elisha; and when the man . . . <u>touched the bones of Elisha, he revived and stood on his feet</u>.
(Bones have a significance far beyond their physical nature.)

Gen 2:23-24 And Adam said: "This is now <u>bone of my bones and flesh of my flesh</u>; she shall be called Woman, because she was taken out of Man." Therefore a man shall leave his father and mother and <u>be joined</u> to his wife, and they shall become <u>one flesh</u>.

1Cor 6:17 But he who is <u>joined</u> {glued} to the Lord is one spirit with Him.

Eph 5:32	This {marriage} is a great mystery, but I speak concerning Christ and the church. **(Marriage is an illustration of two people, their spirits and bodies being made gloriously one. In the same way you are joined to Me.)**
Eph 5:30	<u>For we are members of His body, of His flesh and of His bones.</u> **I delight in being <u>fused into His body</u>, into His flesh and <u>into His bones</u>.** (This goes beyond even a marriage union, your bones are fused into Mine, Your bones the essence of your body, are now energized by My DNA, saturated with My anointing.)

My body is his body

1Cor 6:19-20	Or do you not know that <u>your body is the temple of the Holy Spirit</u> who is in you, whom you have from God, and <u>you are not your own</u>? ... **My body is not my own, it belongs to Him—glory!** (This truth rejoices your heart, because you know I love you perfectly, 1John 4:18.)
John 3:13	"No one has ascended to heaven but He who came down from heaven that is <u>the Son of Man who is in heaven</u>."
Eph 2:6	And raised us up together, and made us sit together in the heavenly places in Christ Jesus, **I delight in living both here and in heaven at the same time** (The life, the promptings you are receiving from Me (including the Word) are greater than, have dominion over, what you are experiencing in the physical world.)
Col 3:4	When <u>Christ who is our life</u> appears, then you also will appear with Him in glory.
Acts 17:28	"for in Him we live and move and have our being, ...

I delight in the glorious truth that He is my life
(Like when you eat rice, it is transformed by your body to become part of your living flesh, so your body, as a living sacrifice, Rom 12:1, is absorbed into My Life.)

John 12:26 If anyone serves Me, let him follow Me, and where I am, there My servant will be also.
I delight that my body is His body—wherever I go, in fact He goes
(I did not say 'where you are, there I will be also'. No—'where I am there My servant will be also'!)

Is 6:3 And one cried to another and said: "Holy, holy, holy is the LORD of hosts; the whole earth is full of His glory!"
1Cor 2:10 But God has revealed them to us through His Spirit. For the Spirit searches all things, yes, the deep things of God.
My eyes are His eyes
(You see My glory in all things—even if at present not visible to the natural eyes.)

John 8:26, 28 . . ." I speak to the world those things which I heard from Him" . . . .
. . . . "I do nothing of Myself; but as My Father taught Me, I speak these things."
My mouth is His mouth
(You hear from Me. The words you speak are also prompted by Me, they too are alive . . . .)

John 5:19 . . . "Most assuredly, I say to you, the Son can do nothing of Himself, but what He sees the Father do; for whatever He does, the Son also does in like manner.
John 14:12 "Most assuredly, I say to you, he who believes in Me, the works that I do he will do also; and greater works than these he will do, because I go to My Father."
I do as he does, even greater things (There is so much more . . . . !)

1John 4:17 **. . . . as He is, so are we in this world**

6

IN HIM—LIVING IN HIS REST

Resting in Him, in Jesus

Heb 4:10 . . . he who has entered His rest has himself also ceased from his works as God did from His.

(It is now natural for you to do as I did as it is natural for a dog to bark.)

We are coming to know deep within that we are hidden in Him, in the three areas we have been digesting, soul, spirit and body:

Soul— We are fused, have become one with the glory in the living Word; we are epistles, 2Cor 3:2-3

Spirit— We are energized by His divine power.

Body— Our bodies are His body.

Therefore, **as He is so are we in this world** which means that we are what He is. What is He like?

John 1:1-4, 14 In the beginning was the Word, and the Word was with God, and the Word was God. He was in the beginning with God. All things were made through Him, and without Him nothing was made that was made. In Him was life, and the life was the light of men. And the Word became flesh and dwelt among us, and we beheld His glory, the glory as of the only begotten of the Father, full of grace and truth.

Heb 1:3	{Jesus} being the brightness of His glory and the express image of His person,
Col 1:19	For it pleased [the Father] that all the divine fullness (the <u>sum total of the divine perfection, powers</u>, and <u>attributes</u>) should dwell in him permanently. AMP
Col 2:9-10	For in Him dwells all the fullness of the Godhead bodily; and <u>you are complete in Him</u> . . .
John 3:34	For He whom God had sent speaks the words of God, for God does not give the Spirit by measure.

No separation, releasing 'Life' from within
This rest takes us beyond knowing who we are, into <u>being who we are</u>.

We have ceased trying to become like Him, eg: to know God's love through our own efforts, which is doomed to failure as it steps into the law. Nor do we say, **I** possess that love. It is in **me**. As long as we retain a sense of **'I'**, a gap can emerge between our experience and God, which gives the enemy access to bring doubt. 'Are you sure?' No, that door is closed. **This rest**, this oneness, this fusion, <u>involves **being that love**</u>, it is who we are, so our lives naturally express it. There is no separation. We are love. If we want more to be evident, knowing it is within, we pray, 'Let more be released', and the Holy Spirit will delight to do this! Jesus declared who He was, eg: 'I am the resurrection and the life', John 11:25. Lazarus was not raised from the dead because Jesus had a specific gift enabling Him to bring the dead to life, but because His life was an expression of who He was, in this case, the resurrection and the life.

Equally He was the perfection of all the glorious Divine qualities of love, peace, joy, wisdom, truth, grace, dominion, authority etc. He could only give what was living within Him. Thus, when He said I give you My peace, authority, joy, He was those characteristics in their perfection. He could have said, I am joy, I am peace, I am authority, I am grace . . . . His life was an expression of them. As He is so are we!!! **We have sought to do as He did, not realising that what He did was an outflowing of those perfect characteristics vibrant within Him**, <u>which we have in us—as He is so are we.</u>

Now <u>'we'</u> are what **He** is!

Thus, we should be making the same declarations He made. (With the exception of the specific ones related to His specific calling as our

Saviour, like 'the Lamb of God who takes away the sin of the world!' John 1:29. For example, only He could say, 'I am the door' John 10:9) Yet something within draws back from saying, "I am love", or "I am the resurrection and the life". I have found an excellent way of getting round this. The bible says we are 'workers together with Him', 2Cor 6:1. We are familiar with the picture of being married to Him, Jer 3:14. When a married couple are going to some place they may say 'we' will come . . . ie: both of them. In the same way, I can refer to myself as 'we', me and the Holy Spirit. Further benefits. If it is 'we' who are evangelising, going to be visiting an awkward person, or preaching in a crusade, there is no place for either fear or pride as He is obviously the dominant one. He has opened the door. I am just hanging in there!

Thus we can say, **'<u>we are</u>'** what Jesus said He was.

We can boldly declare with Him

John 8:12 ". . . I am the light of the world."
(Matt 5:14 "You are the light of the world")
'<u>We</u>' are the light of the world
(Light shines from your eyes, from your innermost being.)

John 6:48 "I am the bread of life."
'<u>We</u>' are the bread of life
(Your life is the living Word. It is expressed and imparted in all you think and do and speak, so others feed from the living Word flowing from you!)

John 11:25 "I am the resurrection and the life."
'<u>We</u>' are the resurrection and the life
(Miracles flow as you are a sign and wonder, Is 8:18.)

<u>Much more</u>

All **His** <u>perfect</u> attributes are within, even if not now totally evident to others! But, as we declare these truths, our spirit dances with joy as it enables the Holy Spirit to make them a reality. If **He** is love, the truth is, 'we' are love! If **He** is peace, 'we' are peace!

Rom 5:5 Now hope does not disappoint, because the love of God has been poured out in our hearts by the Holy Spirit who was given to us.

So we can declare:
'We' are love
(This is not a limited love that seeks return, no it is Divine, zealous , full, unconditional. Don't restrain it.)

John 15:11 These things I have spoke to you, that <u>My joy may remain in you</u>, and that your joy may be full.

John 17:13 . . . and these things I speak in the world, that they may have My joy fulfilled in themselves.

1Pet 1:8-9 whom having not seen you love. Though now you do not see Him, yet believing, you rejoice with joy inexpressible and full of glory,
'We' are joy
(My joy is deep within you. It is the fruit of our beautiful relationship, irrespective of circumstances.)

John 14:27 "Peace I leave with you, My peace I give to you; not as the world gives do I give to you.
'We' are peace
(Rest in total confidence, absolute trust in Me, the Living Word. Worry is foreign to you, Matt 6:25.**)**

John 1:16 And of His fullness we have all received, and grace for grace. {Grace—'charis', comes from 'chairo'—to rejoice. It causes rejoicing—the unmerited favour, undeserved blessing.}

Rom 5:17 . . . those who <u>receive abundance of grace</u> and of the gift of righteousness will reign in life through the One, Jesus Christ.
'We' are grace
(Your whole being is saturated with knowledge of My love, favour, abilities — it causes such joy — it overflows.)

Col 2:3	in whom are hidden all the treasures of wisdom and knowledge.
1Cor 1:30	But <u>of Him you are in Christ Jesus, who became for us wisdom from God</u>—and righteousness and sanctification and redemption—

'We' are wisdom

(Continually prompted by Me, so that you are always at the right place, say and do the right things.)

Josh 1:3	<u>Every place</u> that the sole of your foot will tread upon <u>I have given you</u> . . .
Luke 10:19	"Behold, I give you the authority to trample on serpents and scorpions, and over all the power of the enemy, and nothing shall by any means hurt you.

'We' are authority

(Know that no demon can survive when you tell it to go, James 4:7. **Darkness flees when light is turned on. Indeed in your Presence they quake. Sickness, fear, depression are things of the past.)**

Gen 2:7	And the LORD God . . . breathed into his nostrils the breath of life, and man became a living being {One translation—'another speaking spirit'}.
Prov 18:21	Death and life are in the power of the tongue . . .
John 6:63	It is the Spirit Who gives life, [He is the Life-giver] . . . The words that I speak to you are spirit, and they are life.

'We'—our words, are life (or death)

(Know that as you speak from the spirit, your words create whatever you say. As you say 'peace', peace is created, 'heal', healing power is released . . .)

Rom 12:3	. . . God has dealt to each one a measure of faith {Divine faith}.
2Cor 4:13	And since we have <u>the same spirit</u> of faith . . . .
Mark 11:22	So Jesus answered and said to them, "Have faith in God" {Lit: 'Have the God kind of faith'}

'We' are faith

(Perfect faith, no trace of doubt or unbelief, but rooted in a glorious confidence in Me and in the Word; that we are One, joined in a vital union, inseparable. What you see, hear or feel is irrelevant.)

Luke 4:18	The Spirit of the LORD is upon Me, because He has anointed Me to preach the gospel to the poor; He has sent Me to heal the brokenhearted, to proclaim liberty to the captives and recovery of sight to the blind, to set at liberty those who are oppressed;
1John 2:27	But the anointing which you have received from Him abides in you . . .

'We' are the anointing
(The fullness of My Presence that breaks every yoke.)

John 17:22	"And the glory which You gave Me I have given them, that they may be one just as We are one."

'We' are His glory
(You are a life-giving spirit. Others see My glory in you, and are drawn to Me!)

John 7:38	He who believes in Me, as the Scripture has said, <u>out of his heart will flow rivers of living water</u>.
Ez 47:9	And it shall be that every living thing that moves, wherever the rivers go, will live. There will be a very great multitude of fish, because these waters go there; for they will be healed, and <u>everything will live wherever the river goes</u>.
Rev 22:1-2	And He showed me a pure river of water of life, clear as crystal, proceeding from the throne of God and of the Lamb . . . on either side of the river, was the tree of life, which bore twelve fruits, each tree yielding its fruit every month. The leaves of the tree were for the healing of the nations.

'We' are the resurrection and the life

(Glory—you are the river of life, bringing My life wherever you go . . .nations are impacted.)

7

RESPOND – JUST AS JESUS DID

'We' are one with Him as He was with His Father, John 10:30. 'We' are here to continue His work, to make earth like heaven. The perfection of heaven is our measure. There is no power greater on earth than the love of God burning in and through a human heart. So 'we' 'naturally' <u>respond</u> to situations as He did.

John 10:30   I and My Father are one.
John 17:22   And the glory which You gave Me I have given them, that they may be One just as <u>We</u> are one.

'We' know that we do not have a gift independent of ourselves. 'We' release what we are. Because 'we' are love, that love flows. Because 'we' are authority 'we' know the enemy trembles at our presence and is terrified when 'we' speak. Because 'we' are the resurrection and the life 'we' release life, raising the dead etc. **O the joy of being life-giving spirits, releasing it, giving life to the 'dead', imparting what 'we' are**—transforming lives, changing circumstances!

<u>'We' have absolute confidence that His Life will flow from within</u>

John 4:10   Jesus answered and said to her, "If you knew the gift of God, and who it is who says to you, 'Give Me a drink,' you would have asked Him, and He would have given you living water."
'We' delight in taking every opportunity to speak and manifest this glorious Kingdom

John 8:6-8   . . . Jesus stooped down and wrote on the ground with his finger, as though He did not hear . . . "He who is without sin among you, let him throw a stone at her first."
And again He stooped down and wrote on the ground.
Then those who heard it, being convicted by their conscience, went out one by one . . . .
'We' are kings, 'we' set the standards—those of the Kingdom of God.
(Our heart beating with compassion for them all.)

Rom 4:17   (as it is written, "I have made you a father of many nations") in the presence of Him whom he believed—God, <u>who gives life to the dead and calls those things which do not exist as though they did</u>.

Mark 10:27   But Jesus looked at them and said, "With men it is impossible, but not with God; for with God all things are possible."
'We' are functioning as Jesus did, as true sons of God, He being the firstborn.
(I have called and equipped you to live as I did. You know you are a supernatural being. Our heart is burning with Divine love. We are destroying the works of the enemy and speaking into existence the Kingdom of God. Nothing is impossible for us!)

Hallelujah—as He is so are 'we' in this world!

The impact of these revelations

My True Identity

" . . . they are pure gold! They put into words all the things I felt the Lord was trying to lead me into, and now I just long to bring others into that wonderful place of freedom you spoke with wisdom . . . . This is a fresh experience . . . leaving behind religious bondage and thriving in the truth of His Word.
"Thank you for your ministry. From time to time I turn on Revelation TV hoping you may be speaking words of encouragement . . . ."

Gina Watson
Frinton-on-Sea.

The book, My True Identity, has transformed many lives of people in Zambia, through Apostle Harriet Sleigh. Since she extended her Ministry called Kingdom Life Revival to Zambia. The Spirit of God transformed me to a new way of life during her Burning Bush Cell Group program at Kazembe. This program has grown greatly, to cover nearly every corner of the unreached places in Zambia. People are transformed; filled with the Holy Spirit, they lead others to Christ Jesus and heal the sick.

This movement has covered four provinces in Zambia, Luapula, Northern, North and Eastern Provinces. And we are going to the North Western Province next week. There are so many exciting testimonies and miracles of God. So far we have about 30,010 cell groups formed and 1123 new churches, with about 604 trained Pastors.

This fire is going to other places of unreached people (we need more prayers and support). We have a Bible college built in a permanent structure. So many want to attend the 3 months 'revival' course.

Pastor Z. Mwansa, Principal
Kingdom Life Revival College
Zambia

In Him . . . so much MORE!

'Apostle Harriet has given us a view from our 'heavenly places in Christ Jesus' to see the life of Power that God has prepared for us through Grace from His Almighty Word. God's revelations are brought to us in this book so that 'as He is so are we'—now! We are born of the Spirit who resonates with us as we meditate and live, love and thrive in God's Word, totally intoxicated by the aroma and rivers of the God given Life pulsating through our bodies. God's revelations—God's Word—God's Power, will change your life forever—to sit with Him in eternal fellowship and purpose! Praise God!'

Graham Jeavons
Chelmsford

<u>I read this book, and it has blessed me so much. Inspirational, anointed, revelation, edifying and scripturally accurate are just a few words I would use to describe this wonderful book. I highly recommend it.</u>

Evangelist Trevor Irwin
Philadelphia Mission
London